RASHI

"As for the wise, their body alone perishes in this world."

(*Rashi, on Psalm xlix. 11.*)

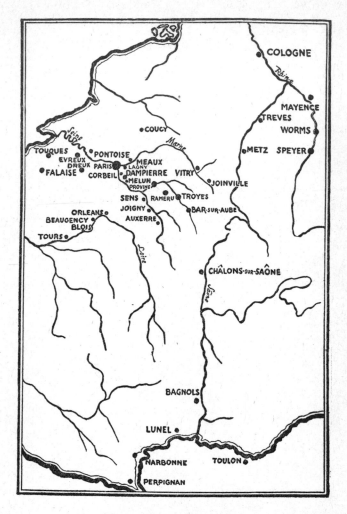

THE RASHI COUNTRY

RASHI

BY

MAURICE LIBER

TRANSLATED FROM THE FRENCH

BY

ADELE SZOLD

PHILADELPHIA

THE JEWISH PUBLICATION SOCIETY OF AMERICA

5706–1945

Copyright, 1906, by

THE JEWISH PUBLICATION SOCIETY OF AMERICA

Reprinted 1945

PRINTED IN THE UNITED STATES OF AMERICA
PRESS OF THE JEWISH PUBLICATION SOCIETY
PHILADELPHIA, PENNA.

TO THE MEMORY OF
ZADOC KAHN
GRAND-RABBIN OF FRANCE

PREFACE

Some months ago the Jewish world celebrated the eight hundredth anniversary of the death of Rashi, who died at Troyes in 1105. On that occasion those whose knowledge authorizes them to speak gave eloquent accounts of his life and work. Science and devotion availed themselves of every possible medium — lectures and books, journals and reviews — to set forth all we owe to the illustrious Rabbi. The writer ventures to express the hope that in the present volume he has made at least a slight contribution toward discharging the common debt of the Jewish nation — that it is not utterly unworthy of him whose name it bears.

This volume, however, is not a product of circumstances; it was not written on the occasion of the centenary celebration. It was designed to form one of the series of the biographies of Jewish Worthies planned by THE JEWISH PUBLICATION SOCIETY OF AMERICA, the first issue of which was devoted to Maimonides. The biography of Rashi is the second of the series. It is not for the author to endorse the order adopted, but he hazards the opinion that the readers will find the portrait of Rashi no unfitting companion-piece even to that of the author of the *Moreh*.

Jewish history may include minds more brilliant and works more original than Rashi's. But it is incontestable that he is one of those historical personages

who afford a double interest; his own personality is
striking and at the same time he is the representative
of a civilization and of a period. He has this double
interest for us to an eminent degree. His physiognomy
has well-marked, individual features, and yet he is the
best exponent of French Judaism in the middle ages.
He is somebody, and he represents something. Through
this double claim, he forms an integral part of Jewish
history and literature. There are great men who despite
their distinguished attributes stand apart from the general intellectual movements. They can be estimated
without reference to an historical background. Rashi
forms, so to say, an organic part of Jewish history. A
whole department of Jewish literature would be enigmatical without him. Like a star which leaves a track
of light in its passage across the skies, Rashi aroused
the enthusiasm of his contemporaries, but no less was
he admired and venerated by posterity, and to-day, after
the lapse of eight centuries, he is, as the poet says, "still
young in glory and immortality."

His name is most prominently connected with rabbinical literature. Whether large questions are dealt
with, or the minutest details are considered, it is always
Rashi who is referred to — he has a share in all its
destinies, and he seems inseparable from it forever.

It is this circumstance that makes the writing of his
biography as awkward a task for the writer as reading
it may be for the public. To write it one must be a
scholar, to read it a specialist. To know Rashi well is as
difficult as it is necessary. Singularly enough, popular
as he was, he was essentially a Talmudist, and at no time
have connoisseurs of the Talmud formed a majority.

This is the reason why historians like Graetz, though they dilate upon the unparalleled qualities of Rashi's genius, can devote only a disproportionately small number of pages to him and his works.

Though the writer has throughout been aware of the difficulties inherent in his task, yet he is also conscious that he has sometimes succeeded in removing them only by eluding them. In parts, when the matter to be treated was unyielding, it became necessary to dwell on side issues, or fill up gaps and replace obscurities by legends and hypotheses. The object in view being a book popular in character and accessible to all, technical discussions had to be eschewed. Many knotty points had to be brushed aside lightly, and the most debatable points passed over in silence. These are the sacrifices to which one must resign himself, though it requires self-restraint to do it consistently. The reader may, therefore, not expect to find new data in these pages, new facts and texts not published before. If the book has any merit, it is that it presents the actual state of knowledge on the subject, and the author anticipates the charge of plagiarism by disclaiming any intention of producing an original work. Recondite sources have not always been referred to, in order not to overload a text which at best is apt to tax the reader's powers of attention. Such references and special remarks as were deemed necessary have been incorporated either in Notes placed at the end of the book, or in an Appendix containing a bibliography. There the works are mentioned to which the author is chiefly indebted, and which his readers may profitably consult if they desire to pursue the subject further.

The author desires to express his appreciation of the work of the translator, whose collaboration was all the more valuable as the revision of the book had to be made, after an interval of almost two years, under most unfavorable conditions, aggravated by the distance between the writer and the place of publication. The readers will themselves judge of the skill with which the translator has acquitted herself of her task, and the author gladly leaves to her the honor and the responsibility for the translation.

But how can I express all I owe to Mr. Israël Lévi, my honored master? Without him this work would never have been begun, without him I should never have dared carry it to completion. I have contracted a debt toward him which grows from day to day, and I discharge but the smallest portion of it by dedicating this volume to the memory of his never-to-be-forgotten father-in-law, the Grand-Rabbin Zadoc Kahn. M. Zadoc Kahn made a name for himself in Jewish letters by his *Etudes sur le livre de Joseph le Zélateur*, dealing with one of the most curious domains of that literature in which Rashi was the foremost representative. One of his last public acts was the appeal which he issued on the occasion of the Rashi centenary. It is not a slight satisfaction to me to know that these pages passed under his eyes in manuscript.

M. LIBER

CHÂLONS–SUR–MARNE, March, 1906

CONTENTS

PREFACE
(page 3)

INTRODUCTION
(page 13)

BOOK I—RASHI THE MAN

CHAPTER I

THE JEWS OF FRANCE IN THE ELEVENTH CENTURY

CHAPTER II

THE YOUTH AND EDUCATION OF RASHI

INTRODUCTION

A people honors itself in honoring the great men who have interpreted its thought, who are the guardians of its genius. It thus renders merited homage and pays just tribute to those who have increased the treasures of its civilization, and added a new feature to its moral physiognomy; it establishes the union of ideas that assures the conservation of the national genius, and maintains and perpetuates the consciousness of the nation. Finally, it manifests consciousness of its future in taking cognizance of its past, and, in turning over the leaves of its archives, it defines its part and mission in history. The study of men and facts in the past permits of a sounder appreciation of recent efforts, of present tendencies; for "humanity is always composed of more dead than living," and usually "the past is what is most vital in the present."

No people has greater need than the Jews to steep itself again in the sources of its existence, and no period more than the present imposes upon it the duty of bringing its past back to life. Scattered over the face of the globe, no longer constituting a body politic, the Jewish people by cultivating its intellectual patrimony creates for itself an ideal fatherland; and mingled, as it is, with its neighbors, threatened by absorption into surrounding nations, it recovers a sort of individuality by the reverence it pays to men that have given best expression to its peculiar genius.

But the Jewish people, its national life crushed out of it, though deprived of all political ambitions, has yet regained a certain national solidarity through community of faith and ideals; and it has maintained the cohesion of its framework by the wholly spiritual bonds of teaching and charity. This is the picture it presents throughout the middle ages, during the period which, for Christianity, marked an eclipse of the intellect and, as it were, an enfeeblement of the reason to such a degree that the term middle ages becomes synonymous with intellectual decadence. "But," said the historian Graetz, "while the sword was ravaging the outer world, and the people devoted themselves to murderous strife, the house of Jacob cared only that the light of the mind burn on steadily and that the shadows of darkness be dissipated. If a religion may be judged by its principal representatives, the palm must be awarded to Judaism in the tenth to the thirteenth century." Its scholars, therefore, its philosophers, and its poets render Judaism illustrious, and by their works and their renown shed a radiant light upon its history.

Maimonides is one of those eminent spirits in whom was reflected the genius of the Jewish people and who have in turn contributed to the development of its genius.[1] Maimonides, however, was also more than this; perhaps he presents as much of interest from the point of view of Arabic as of Jewish culture; and expressing more than the Jewish ideal, he does not belong to the Jews entirely. Of Rashi, on the contrary, one may say that he is a Jew to the exclusion of everything else. He is no more than a Jew, no other than a Jew.

BOOK I

RASHI THE MAN

BOOK I

RASHI THE MAN

CHAPTER I

THE JEWS OF FRANCE IN THE ELEVENTH CENTURY

Great men—and Rashi, as we shall see, may be counted among their number—arrive at opportune times. Sometimes we congratulate them for having disappeared from history in good season; it would be just as reasonable, or, rather, just as unreasonable, to be grateful to them for having come at exactly the right juncture of affairs. The great man, in fact, is the man of the moment; he comes neither too soon, which spares him from fumbling over beginnings and so clogging his own footsteps, nor too late, which prevents him from imitating a model and so impeding the development of his personality. He is neither a precursor nor an epigone, neither a forerunner nor a late-comer. He neither breaks the ground nor gleans the harvest: he is the sower who casts the seed upon a field ready to receive it and make it grow.

It is, therefore, of some avail for us to devote several pages to the history of the Jews of Northern France in the eleventh century, especially in regard to their intellectual state and more especially in regard to their rabbinical culture. If another reason were needed to justify this preamble, I might invoke a principle long ago formulated and put to the test by criticism, namely, that environment is an essential factor in the make-up of a writer, and an intellectual work is always determined, conditioned by existing circumstances. The principle applies to Rashi, of whom one may say, of whom in fact Zunz has said, he is the representative *par excellence* of his time and of his circle.

* * * * * * *

In the great migratory movement beginning at the dawn of the Christian era, which scattered the Jews to the four corners of the globe, and which was accentuated and precipitated by the misfortunes that broke over the population of Palestine, France, or, more exactly, Gaul, was colonized by numbers of Jews. If we believe in the right of the first occupant, we ought to consider the French Jews more French than many Frenchmen. Conversions must at first have been numerous, and the number of apostates kept pace with the progress of Christianity.

In the south of France, there were Jewish communities before the fifth century; in Burgundy and Touraine, in the first half of the sixth century; and in Austrasia, at the end of the same century. From the Provence, they ascended the Rhone and the Saône. Others reached Guienne and Anjou.[2]

Although disturbed at times by the canons of various distrustful Church councils, or by the sermons of a few

vehement bishops, the Jews on the whole led a peaceful,
though not a very prosperous, existence, which has left
scarcely any traces in history and literature. Aside from
a few unimportant names and facts, these centuries mark
a gap in the history of the Jews of France, as in that of
their Christian neighbors; and literature, as it always
does, followed the political and economic destinies of the
nation. From the fifth to the tenth centuries, letters fell
into utter decay, despite the momentary stimulus given
by Charlemagne. The human intellect, to borrow from
Guizot, had reached the nadir of its course. This epoch,
however, was not entirely lost to civilization. The Jews
applied themselves to studies, the taste for which developed more and more strongly. If as yet they could not
fly with their own wings, they remained in relation with
the centres of rabbinical life, the academies in Babylonia, exchanging the products of the mind at the same
time that they bartered merchandise. This slow process
of incubation was perforce fruitful of results.

I

It was in the tenth century, when the political and
social troubles that had agitated Europe since the fall of
the Roman Empire were calmed, that the Jews came
forth from their semi-obscurity, either because their
numbers had increased, or because their position had
become more stable, or because they were ready, after
mature preparation, to play their part in the intellectual
world.

At this time, the Jews of Northern France nearly
without exception enjoyed happy conditions of existence.

From their literature, rather scholarly than popular, we learn chiefly of their schools and their rabbis; yet we also learn from it that their employments were the same as those of the other inhabitants of the country. They were engaged in trade, many attaining wealth; and a number devoted themselves to agriculture. They possessed fields and vineyards, for neither the ownership of land nor residence in the country was forbidden them; and they were also employed in cattle raising. Often they took Christians into their service.

But the Jews, although they attached themselves to the soil and tried to take root there, were essentially an urban population. They owned real estate and devoted themselves to all sorts of industries. They were allowed to be workmen and to practice every handicraft, inasmuch as the guilds, those associations, partly religious in character, which excluded the Jews from their membership rolls, did not begin to be established until the twelfth century. Sometimes a Jew was entrusted with a public office, as a rule that of collector of taxes. Not until later, about the twelfth century, when forced by men and circumstances, did the Jews make a specialty of money-lending..

The strength of the Jews resided in the fact that they were organized in communities, which were marked by intense solidarity, and in which harmony and tranquillity were assured by the rabbinical institutions. Failure to respect these institutions was punished by excommunication—a severe penalty, for the excommunicated man encountered the hate of his co-religionists and was driven to baptism.[3]

At the head of the communities were provosts (*praepositi*), charged with surveillance over their interests, and doubtless their representatives before the civil authority. Many Jews were highly esteemed by the kings or seigneurs, holding positions of honor and bearing honorific titles; but in general the Jews of France, unlike those of Spain, were not permitted to take part in the government, or even have a share in the political life of the nation. They contented themselves with the enjoyment of the fruits of their labor and the peaceful practice of their religion. They were the less disturbed because they lived under a special *régime*. Being neither French nor Christian, they were therefore not citizens; they formed a state within the state, or rather a colony within the state, and, being neither nobles nor serfs, they did not have to render military service. They administered their internal affairs, and in general were not amenable to civil or ecclesiastical legislation. For the solution of their legal difficulties they applied to the rabbinical tribunals. In all other respects they were dependent upon the lord of the lands upon which they established themselves, provided they were not under the *tutelle et mainbournie* of the king. In either case they had to pay taxes and constitute themselves a constantly flowing source of revenues for their protectors.

The Jews lived on a basis of good understanding with their neighbors, and came into frequent intercourse with them. Even the clergy maintained relations with Jewish scholars. It was the incessant efforts of the higher ecclesiastics and of the papacy that little by little created animosity against the Jews, which at the epoch of Rashi was still not very apparent. The collections of canon-

ical law by force of tradition renewed the humiliating
measures prescribed by the last Roman emperors.

The Jews throughout France spoke French; and they
either had French names or gave their Hebrew names a
French form.[4] In the rabbinical writings cities are designated by their real names, or by Hebrew names more or
less ingeniously adapted from the Latin or Romance.
With the secularization of their names, the Jews adopted,
at least partially, the customs and, naturally, also the
superstitions of their countrymen. The valuable re-
searches of Güdemann and Israël Lévi show how much
the folk-lore of the two races have in common. Moreover, when two peoples come in contact, no matter how
great the differences distinguishing them, they are bound
to exert mutual influence upon each other. No imper-
vious partitions exist in sociology.

It would thus be an anachronism to represent the Jews
of the eleventh century as pale and shabby, ever bearing
the look of hunted animals, shamefaced, depressed by
clerical hate, royal greed, and the brutality of the masses.
In the Jewries of France at this time there was nothing
sad or sombre, no strait-laced orthodoxy, no jargon, no
disgraceful costume, none of that gloomy isolation be-
tokening distrust, scorn, and hate.

The practical activity of the Jews, their business
interests, and their consequent wealth did not stifle
intellectual ideals. On the contrary, thanks to the
security assured them, they could devote themselves to
study. Their rich literature proves they could occupy
themselves at the same time with mental and material
pursuits. "For a people to produce scholars, it is
necessary that it be composed of something other than

hard-hearted usurers and sordid business men. The literary output is a thorough test of social conditions."[5] Moreover, the intellectual status of a people always bears relation to its material and economic condition, and so, where the Jews enjoyed most liberty and happiness, their literature has been richest and most brilliant.

From an intellectual point of view the Jews resembled the people among whom they lived. Like them, they were pious, even extremely devout; and they counted few unbelievers among their number. Sometimes it happened that a religious person failed to obey precepts, but no one contested the foundations of belief. In the matter of religion, it is true, outward observance was guarded above everything else. The Jews, settled as they were on foreign soil, came to attach themselves to ceremonials as the surest guarantees of their faith. Naturally superstitions prevailed at an epoch marked by a total lack of scientific spirit. People believed in the existence of men without shadows, in evil demons, and so on. The Jews, however, were less inclined to such conceptions than the Christians, who in every district had places of pilgrimage at which they adored spurious bones and relics.

It would be altogether unjust not to recognize the ethical results of the constant practice of the law, which circumscribed the entire life of the Jew. Talmudic legislation must not be regarded, as it sometimes is, as an oppressive yoke, an insufferable fetter. Its exactions do not make it tyrannical, because it is loyally and freely accepted, accepted even with pleasure. The whole life of the Jew is taken into consideration beforehand, its boundaries are marked, its actions controlled. But this submission entails no self-denial; it is voluntary, and the reason is provided with sufficient motives. Indeed, it is remarkable what freedom and breadth thought was able to maintain in the very bosom of orthodoxy.

"The observance of the Law and, consequently, the study of the Law formed the basis of this religion. With the fall of the Temple the one place disappeared in which the Divine cult could legitimately be performed; as a result the Jews turned for the expression of their religious sentiment with all the more ardor toward the Law, now become the real sanctuary of Judaism torn from its native soil, the safeguard of the wandering race, the one heritage of a glorious and precious past. The recitation and study of the Law took the place of religious ceremonies—hence the name "school" (*Schul*) for houses of worship in France and in Germany. The endeavor was made to give the Law definite form, to develop it, not only in its provisions remaining in practical use, such as the civil and penal code, regulations in regard to the festivals, and private observances, but also in its provisions relating to the Temple cult which had historical interest only. This occupation, pursued with warmth and depth of feeling for a number of centuries, appealed at once to the intellect and the heart. It may be said that the entire Jewish race shared in the work, the scholar being removed from the general mass only in degree, not in kind."[6]

The high level of general instruction among the Jews was all the more remarkable since only a small number of literary works were known. Though copies were made of those which enjoyed the greatest reputation, the number of manuscripts was limited. Nevertheless, soon after their appearance, important productions in one country came into the hands of scholars of other countries. Just as Christendom by force of its spiritual bond formed a single realm, so two strong chains bound together Jews of widely separated regions: these were their religion and their language. Communication was difficult, roads were few in number and dangerous; yet, countervailing distance and danger was devotion to religion and to learning.

But religion and learning were one and the same thing. As was the case in Christianity, and for the same reasons, religion filled the whole of life and engrossed all branches of knowledge. There was no such thing as secular science; religion placed its stamp on everything, and turned the currents of thought into its own channels. One must not hope therefore to find, among the Jews of Northern France, those literary species which blossomed and flourished in Spain; philosophy did not exist among them, and poetry was confined to a few dry liturgic poems. Their intellectual activity was concentrated in the study of the Bible and the Talmud; but in this domain they acquired all the greater depth and penetration. Less varied as were the objects of their pursuits, they excelled in what they undertook, and inferior though they were in the fields of philosophy and poetry, they were superior in Biblical exegesis, and still more so, possibly, in Talmudic jurisprudence.

II

The history of the beginnings of rabbinical learning in France is wrapped in obscurity. Tradition has it that Charlemagne caused the scholar Kalonymos to come from Lucca to Mayence. With his sons he is said to have opened a school there, which became the centre of Talmudic studies in Lorraine. Legends, however slight their semblance to truth, are never purely fictitious in character; they contain an element of truth, or, at least, symbolize the truth; and this tradition, which cannot be accepted in the shape in which it has been

handed down, seeing that Kalonymos lived in the tenth
century, is nevertheless a fairly exact representation
of the continuity of the intellectual movement. If the
fact is not established that Charlemagne accomplished
for the Jews what he did for the Christians, that is,
revived their schools and promoted their prosperity,
it seems more certain that rabbinical learning penetrated
into the northwest of Europe through the intermediation of Italy, which bridged the gap between the Orient
and the Rhine lands.

As is well known, Christian Italy during the early
middle ages, despite the successive invasions of the
barbarians, remained the centre of civilization and the
store-house of Occidental learning. It is in Italy, without doubt, that the Romanesque style of architecture had
its origin, and in Italy that the study of the Roman law
was vigorously resumed. It is to Italy also that Charlemagne turned when he sought for scholars to place at
the head of his schools. Moreover, it was on Italian
soil, in the fifteenth century, that the magnificent blos-
som meriting its name, the Renaissance, was destined
to open and unfold its literary and artistic beauties.

Italy owes its glorious part in the world's history both
to its geographical position and its commercial importance. So likewise with the Jews of Italy, their commercial activities contributed to their intellectual prosperity.
In the ninth century they possessed rabbinical authorities, and in the tenth century, centres of Talmudic study.
At this period, the celebrated family of the Kalonymides
went to Lorraine to establish itself there. For some
time Mayence was the metropolis of Judaism in the
Rhine countries; and by its community the first acade-

mies were established, the first Talmudic commentaries
were composed, and decisions were made which were
accepted by all the Jews of Christian Europe. Soon
this intellectual activity extended to Worms, to Speyer,
and a little later to the western part of Germany and the
northern part of France.[7] A veritable renaissance took
place, parallel with the movement of ideas which went
on in the schools and convents of the eleventh and
fourteen centuries;[8] for Jewish culture is often bound
up with the intellectual destinies of the neighboring
peoples.

For some time the schools of Lorraine stood at the
head of the Talmudic movement, and it was to them that
Rashi came a little later to derive instruction.

One of the most celebrated offspring of the family of
the Kalonymides is Meshullam ben Kalonymos, who
lived at Mayence in the second half of the tenth century.
He was a Talmudist held in high regard and the com-
poser of liturgic poetry. He devoted himself to the
regulation of the material and spiritual affairs of his
brethren. Although he stood in correspondence with the
Babylonian masters, he was in a position to pass judgment independently of them. Communication with the
East was frequent. The communities of France and
Germany sent disciples to the Babylonians and submitted difficulties to them. Tradition relates that the
Gaon Natronaï (about 865) even visited France. However that may be, the Jews of France at an early period
were acquainted with Babylonian works, both the
chronicles and the legal codes.

Other Talmudists of the tenth century are known, but
rabbinical literature may be said to have commenced

only with Gershom ben Judah (about 960–1028). According to tradition his master was his contemporary Haï Gaon; in reality he was the disciple of Judah ben Meïr ha-Cohen, surnamed Leontin (about 975). Originally from Metz, Gershom established himself at Mayence, to which a large number of pupils from neighboring countries soon flocked in order to attend his school. Thus he was the legatee of the Babylonian academies, the decay of which became daily more marked. In his capacity as head of a school as in many other respects, he was the true forerunner of Rashi, who carried on his work with greater command of the subject and with more success.

Rabbenu Gershom not only gave Talmudic learning a fresh impetus and removed its centre to the banks of the Rhine, but he also exerted the greatest and most salutary influence upon the social life of his co-religionists, through his "Decrees," religious and moral, which, partly renewing older institutions, were accepted by all the Jews of Christian countries. Among other things, he forebade polygamy. He merits consideration in two aspects, as a Gaon and as one to whom his disciples gave the surname which still attaches to him, "the Light of the Exile," *Meor ha-Golah*. Rashi said of him: "Rabbenu Gershom has enlightened the eyes of the Captivity; for we all live by his instruction; all the Jews of these countries call themselves the disciples of his disciples."

Gershom seems to have been the first Rhenish scholar who resorted to the written word for the spread of his teachings. He devoted himself to the establishment of a correct text of the Bible and the Talmud, and his chief work is a Talmudical commentary.

Since his time the continuity of learning has been uninterrupted. The seed sown by Rabbenu Gershom was not long in germinating. Schools began to multiply and develop in Lorraine. The one at Mayence prospered for a long time, and was eclipsed only by the schools of Champagne.

A rabbi, Machir, the brother of Gershom, by his Talmudic lexicon contributed likewise to the development of rabbinical knowledge. His four sons were renowned scholars, contemporaries and doubtless fellow-students of Rashi.

The disciples of Gershom, who continued the work of their master, are of especial interest to us, because one of them, Simon the Elder, was the maternal uncle of Rashi, and three others were his masters. These were Jacob ben Yakar, Isaac ha-Levi, and Isaac ben Judah. The latter two were disciples also of Eliezer ben Isaac the Great, of Mayence. Jacob ben Yakar and Isaac ha-Levi went to Worms, where they became rabbis, while Isaac ben Judah remained at Mayence, and directed the Talmudic school there.

About the middle of the eleventh century, then, an intellectual ferment took place in France and Lorraine, earnest literary and scientific activity manifested itself, and above all elements of profound rabbinical culture became visible. But one who should regulate these forces was lacking, a guide to direct these activities and to serve as a model to others. In order that the movement might not come to a premature end, a master was needed who would give it impetus and define its course, who would strike the decisive blow. Such a man there

was, a man who impressed his contemporaries as a
scholar of high degree and noble character, and whose
memory as such is still cherished by posterity. This man
was Rashi.

CHAPTER II

The Youth and Education of Rashi

Little is known concerning the life of Rashi. Owing to various causes not a single work is extant that might be used as a guide for the establishment of minor facts. Generally speaking, Jewish literature in the middle ages was of an impersonal character; practically no memoirs nor autobiographies of this period exist. The disciples of the great masters were not lavish of information concerning them. They held their task to be accomplished when they had studied and handed on the master's works; regard for his teachings ranked above respect for the personality of the author. But the figure of Rashi, as though in despite of all such obstacles, has remained popular. People wanted to know all the details of his life, and they invented facts according to their desires. Fiction, however, fell short of the truth. Legend does not represent him so great as he must actually have been. In the present work, too, I shall be obliged to resort to comparisons and analogies, to supplement by hypotheses the scanty information afforded by history, yet I shall distinguish the few historic facts from the mass of legends in which they are smothered.

As of old many cities in Greece asserted that they were the birthplace of Homer, the national poet, so a number of cities disputed for the honor of being the birthplace

of Rashi, or of having been his residence, or the scene
of his death. Worms claimed him as one of its rabbis,
Lunel, thanks to a confusion of names, has passed as
his birthplace, and Prague as the city of his death.
One historian set 1105 as the year of his birth, though
in fact it is the year of his death. Others placed it in
the thirteenth century, and still others even in the
fourteenth.

In the course of this narrative other such instances
will occur—of fables, more or less ingenious, collected
by chroniclers lacking discrimination. They may make
pleasant reading, although they contain no element of
authenticity. Besides, they are of relatively recent date,
and emanate to a large extent from Italy and Spain,
whose historians could count upon the credulity of their
readers to impose their inventions upon Jews and
Christians alike.

Confusion of this sort reigned in regard to Rashi's life
until 1823, the year in which the illustrious Zunz published the essay which established, not only his own,
but also Rashi's reputation, and brought Rashi forth
from the shadow of legend into the full light of history.

We owe a debt of gratitude to Zunz and other scholars,
such as Geiger, Weiss, Berliner, and Epstein, because,
with the legendary often superimposed upon the true,
they have made it easy to pick out the genuine from the
false. Now that the result of their labors is before us,
no great difficulty attaches to the task of casting off
legend from history, and extracting from the legendary
whatever historic material it contains.

THE RASHI CHAPEL AT WORMS

FROM A PHOTOGRAPH

I

In brushing aside all the myths with which the biography of Rashi is cobwebbed, one finds, not a varied life, rich in incident, but an entirely intellectual life, whose serenity was undisturbed by excitement.

An event dividing Rashi's life into almost equal parts is his taking up his residence at Troyes. During the earlier period he received his education, at first in the city of his birth, then in the academies of Lorraine. On his return to Troyes, he had matured and was thoroughly equipped. In the school he founded there, he grouped pupils about him and wrote the works destined to perpetuate his influence.

First of all, it is necessary to make Rashi's acquaintance, as it were, to know the names he bore and those he did not bear. An example of the fantastic stories of which he was the hero is afforded by the name Yarḥi, which is sometimes still given to him. It does not date further back than the sixteenth century, before which time he was called R. Solomon (Shelomo) by the Jews of France, and R. Salomon ha-Zarfati (the Frenchman) by Jews outside of France. Christian scholars likewise called him R. Salomo Gallicus, and also briefly R. Solomon, as the most celebrated rabbi who ever bore that name. So said Abbé Bartolocci, one of the first and most eminent bibliographers of rabbinical literature, explaining that the short appellation had the same force as when Saint Paul is designated simply as "the apostle."

The usual name applied to Rashi (R Sh I) is formed, in accordance with a well-known Jewish custom, from the initials of his name and patronymic in Hebrew,

Rabbi Shelomo Izḥaki,[9] which the Christians translated
by Solomon Isaacides, just as they made Maimonides of
Moses ben Maimon. Raymond Martini, the celebrated
author of the *Pugio fidei*, seems to have been the first
who saw in Rashi the initials of the words, R. Solomon
Yarḥi. He confused Rashi either with a Solomon of
Lunel, mentioned by the traveller Benjamin of Tudela,
or with a grammarian, Solomon ben Abba Mari, of
Lunel, who lived in the second half of the fourteenth
century. Sebastian Münster, the German Hebraist
(1489–1552), and the elder Buxtorf (1564–1629),
the humanist and highly esteemed Hebrew scholar,
popularized the mistake, which soon gave rise to another. L'Empereur, also a scholar in Hebraica, of
the seventeenth century, went even further than his
predecessors, in holding Lunel[10] to have been the birthplace of Rashi, while Basnage (1653–1725), the celebrated historian of the Jews, spoke of "Solomon the
Lunatic."

Though as early a writer as Richard Simon (1638–
1712) protested against the error of making Lunel the
native city of Rashi, the mistake crept even into Jewish
circles. Since this city of Languedoc was one of the
principal centres of Jewish learning in the Provence
during the middle ages, Rashi, in most unexpected
fashion, came to swell the number of "scholars" of
Lunel, of whom mention is frequently made in rabbinical
literature. It even seems that at the beginning of the
nineteenth century, Jews of Bordeaux went to Lunel
on a pilgrimage to his tomb.

In point of fact Rashi was neither a German nor a
Provençal; he was born and he died in Champagne, at
Troyes. At that time France was divided into a dozen

distinct countries, one of the most important of which was the countship of Champagne, to the northeast, between the Ile-de-France and Lorraine. There were Jews in all the important localities of the province, especially in the commercial cities. In the period with which we are dealing, fairs took place every year successively at Lagny, Bar-sur-Aube, Provins, Troyes, and again Provins and Troyes. The principal city was Troyes, which at the end of the ninth century, when it contained about twelve thousand inhabitants, was chosen as their capital by the counts of Champagne.

In a wide plain, where the Seine divides into several branches, rises the city of Troyes, maintaining to some extent its medieval character, with its narrow ill-paved streets, which of old swarmed with geese and porkers, and with its houses of wooden gables and overhanging roofs. Manufactures prospered at Troyes. Many tanneries were established there, and parchment was exported from all parts of the district. In fact it has been suggested that the development of the parchment industry at Troyes furthered the literary activity for which the province was noted, by providing writing material at a time when in general it was so rare. But manufactures in that period had not attained a high degree of perfection, and the main instrument for obtaining wealth was commerce, chiefly the commerce carried on at fairs, those great lists periodically opened to the commercial activity of a whole province or a whole country. Troyes, celebrated for its fairs, was the scene of two a year, one beginning on St. John's Day (the warm fair), and one beginning on St. Remy's Day (the cold fair). They covered a quarter so important that it constituted two large parishes by itself.

Although religion had already begun to intervene in the regulation of the fairs, Jews took a large part in them, and somewhat later, like the Jews of Poland in the seventeenth century, they used them as the occasions for rabbinical synods. In the Jewish sources, the fairs of Troyes are frequently mentioned. The relations that sprang up among the great number of Jews that went to them were favorable to the cause of science, since the Jews in pursuing their material interests did not forget those of learning. Thus the fairs exercised a certain influence upon the intellectual movement.

Troyes was also the seat of a permanent Jewish community of some importance; for a Responsum of the first half of the eleventh century declared that the regulations of the community should have the force of law for each member, and when the regulations deal with questions of general import they were to hold good for neighboring communities as well. Another Responsum dating from the same period shows that the Jews of France owned land and cultivated the vine. Troyes no longer bears visible traces of the ancient habitation of the Jews. It is possible that the parish of St. Frobert occupies the ground covered by the old Jewry; and probably the church of St. Frobert, now in ruins, and the church of St. Pantaléon were originally synagogues. But in Rashi's works there are more striking evidences that Jews were identified with Troyes. Certain of his expressions or other indications attach them to the city of Troyes, "our city," as he says.

Rashi, then, was born at Troyes in 1040—the year of
Gershom's death, some authors affirm, who are more
concerned with the pragmatism of history than its truth,
more with scientific continuity than with the sequence
of events. But if it is almost certain that the rabbi,
who, as I said, was the precursor of Rashi, had been
dead for twelve years, 1040 (possibly 1038) is probably
the year of the death of another authority, no less
celebrated, Haï Gaon, whose passing away marks the
irreparable decadence of the Babylonian Gaonate. The
French rabbi and his Spanish colleagues were destined to
harvest the fruits of this Gaonate and carry on its work,
exemplifying the words of the Talmud: "When one
star is extinguished in Israel, another star rises on the
horizon."

In order that Rashi should have a setting in accord
with so high a position, legend has surrounded his family
with a nimbus of glory. History, it is true, does not
make mention of his ancestors, and this silence, joined
to the popularity which Rashi came to enjoy, inspired,
or was an added stimulus to, the fantastic genealogic
theories of those who in their admiration of him, or
through pride of family, declared him to have been
descended from a rabbi of the third century, Johanan
ha-Sandlar.[11] All that can be said with certainty is,
that his maternal uncle was Simon the Elder, a disciple of Gershom and a learned and respected rabbi.
Rashi's father Isaac appears to have been well-educated.
Rashi on one occasion mentions a certain bit of instruction he had received from him. Tradition, fond
of ascribing illustrious ancestors to its heroes, would
see in this Isaac one who through his knowledge and

godliness deserved to share in the renown of his son, and to whom his son, moreover, rendered pious homage by quoting him in the opening passage[12] of the commentary on Genesis. We would willingly believe Rashi capable of a delicate attention of this kind, only we know that the Isaac cited is a certain Talmudic scholar.

Tradition, letting its fancy play upon the lives of great men, delights also in clothing their birth with tales of marvels. Sometimes the miraculous occurs even before they are born and points to their future greatness. The father of Rashi, for instance, is said to have possessed a precious gem of great value. Some Christians wanted to take it away from him, either because they desired to put it to a religious use, or because they could not bear the sight of such a treasure in the hands of a Jew. Isaac obstinately refused their offers. One day the Christians lured him into a boat, and demanded that he give up his gem. Isaac, taking a heroic stand, threw the object of their ardent desires into the water. Then a mysterious voice was heard in his school pronouncing these words: "A son will be born to thee, O Isaac, who will enlighten the eyes of all Israel." According to a less familiar tradition, Isaac lived in a seaport town, where he earned a poor livelihood as stevedore. Once he found a pearl in the harbor, and went in all haste to show it to his wife, the daughter of a jeweler. Realizing the value of the pearl, she could not contain herself, and went forthwith to a jeweler. He offered her ten thousand ducats, double its value, because the duke was anxious to buy it as an adornment for the bishop's cope. The woman would not listen to the proposition, and ran back to her husband to tell him to what use the pearl was going to be put. Rather than have it adorn a bishop's vestment, Isaac threw it into the sea, sacrificing his fortune to his God.

The scene of another tradition is laid at Worms. One day his wife, who had become pregnant, was walking along a street of the city when two carriages coming from opposite directions collided. The woman in danger of being crushed pressed up close against a wall, and the wall miraculously sank inward to make way for her. This made Isaac fear an accusation of witchcraft, and he left Worms for Troyes, where a son was born to him, whom he named Solomon.

To turn from the mythical to the hypothetical—the young Solomon probably received his early education in his own family, and what this education was, can easily be conceived. It was the duty of the father himself to take charge of the elementary instruction of his son and turn the first glimmerings of the child's reason upon the principles of religion. This instruction was concentrated upon the observance of laws and customs. "From the tenderest age," says Dr. M. Berliner, "the child was initiated into the observance of religious precepts, and was put upon his guard against their transgression. His parents had but one aim, to inculcate in him the religion of his ancestors and render the Law, the source of this religion, accessible to him. He was thus inured to the struggle of life, in which his shield was belief in God. The mother also took part in the rearing of her child. Her lullabies were often prayers or Biblical hymns, and although the women, as a rule, did not receive a thorough education, they effectually helped to make observant devotees of the Law of their children."[13] Five or six was the age at which Hebrew was begun to be taught to the child, and the occasion was usually celebrated by a picturesque ceremony full of poetic feeling. On the morning of the Pentecost, the festival which commemorates the giving of the Law on Mt. Sinai, or on the morning of the Rejoicing of the Law, the day devoted above all others to honoring the Law, the child, dressed in his holiday clothes and wrapped in a Tallit, was led to the synagogue by his father or by a scholar who acted as sponsor. In the synagogue the child listened to the reading of the Law; then he was led to the house of the teacher to whom his education was to be entrusted. The teacher took him in his arms, "as a nursing-father carrieth the sucking child," and presented him with a tablet, on which were written the Hebrew alphabet and some verses from the Bible applicable to the occasion. The tablet was then spread with honey, which the child ate as if to taste the sweetness of the Law of God. The child was also shown a bun made by a young maiden, out of flour kneaded together with milk and with oil or honey, and bearing among other inscriptions the words of Ezekiel: "Son of man, cause thy belly to eat, and fill thy bowels with this roll that I give thee. Then did I eat it; and it was in my mouth as honey for sweetness." Other Biblical passages were inscribed on the shell of an egg, and after they were read, the bun and the egg as well as apples and other fruit were eaten by the pupils present.

This ceremony, marred only by the introduction of superstitious practices, such as the conjuring up of evil demons, was well adapted to stamp itself on the child's mind, and its naïve symbolism was bound to make a profound impression upon his imagination. Pagan antiquity knew of nothing so delicate and at the same time so elevated in sentiment. Pindar, and Horace after him, conceived the fancy that the bees of Hymettus alighted on the child's brow and dropped rich honey upon it. The Jewish celebration of a new period in childhood, though not a poetic fiction, is none the less charming and picturesque. It shows how precious was the cultivation of the mind to a people whom the world delights to represent as absorbed by material interests and consumed by the desire for wealth. Education has always been highly valued among the Jews, who long acted up to the saying of Lessing: "The schoolmaster holds the future in his hands." The religious law is a system of instruction, the synagogue is a school. It will redound to the eternal honor of Judaism that it raised the dissemination of knowledge to the height of a religious precept. At a time when among the Christians knowledge was the special privilege of the clergy, learning was open to every Jew, and, what is still finer, the pursuit of it was imposed upon him as a strict obligation. The recalcitrant, say the legalists, is compelled to employ a tutor for his child. Every scholar in Israel is obliged to gather children about him; and the rabbinical works contain most detailed recommendations concerning the organization of schools and methods of instruction. One comes upon principles and rules of pedagogy unusually advanced for their time. For instance, teachers were forbidden to have more than forty pupils, and were not to use a more severe means of punishment than whipping with a small strap. In Christian schools, on the contrary, pedagogic methods were backward and barbarous.

It was considered an excellent plan to beat all pupils with the ferrule, in order to make knowledge enter the heads of the bad and to keep the good from the sin of pride.

Among the Jews instruction was tempered to suit the faculty of the learner. First the child was taught to read Hebrew, translate the daily prayers, and recite the more important of them by heart. Then the Pentateuch beginning with Leviticus was explained to him, and, if necessary, it was translated into French. It was read with a special chant. Rashi, be it said parenthetically, by his commentary gave this Bible instruction a more solid basis. Not until the pupil was a little older did he study the Talmud, which is so well qualified to develop intelligence and clear-headedness. His elementary education completed, and provided he had shown taste and inclination for the more difficult studies, the young man went to special schools. But if he had not shown signs of progress, he was taught simply to read Hebrew and understand the Bible.

The author of a curious pedagogic regulation in the middle ages fixes the whole term of study at fourteen years: the seven years preceding the religious majority of the child are spent in the local school, at the study of the Pentateuch (two years), at the study of the rest of the Bible (two years), and at the study of the easier Talmudic treatises (three years). The remaining seven years are devoted to the higher study of the Talmud in an academy outside the birthplace of the youth. This education was obtained sometimes from private teachers, and sometimes in schools founded and maintained at the expense of the community or even of educational societies.

A sufficiently clear idea may thus be obtained of Rashi's early education; and in assuming that he soon distinguished himself for precocity and for maturity of thought, we shall not be shooting wide of the mark. But legend will not let its heroes off so cheaply; legend will have it that Rashi, in order to complete his education, travelled to the most distant lands. Not satisfied with having him go to the south of France, to Narbonne, to the school of Moses ha-Darshan (who had doubtless died before Rashi's coming to his school was a possibility), or to Lunel, to attend the school of Zerahiah ha-Levi (not yet born), tradition maintains that at the age of thirty-three Rashi made the tour of almost the whole world as then known, in order to atone for a mistake made by his father, who regretted having lost a precious object, and also in order to assure himself that his commentaries had not been surpassed. He is said to have traversed Italy, Greece, Egypt, Palestine, and Persia, returning by way of Germany.

So long a voyage must, of course, have been marked by a number of events. In Egypt, Rashi became the disciple—the more exigent say, the intimate friend—of Maimonides, who, as we all know, was born in 1135, nearly a century later than Rashi. Maimonides, as fiction recounts, conceived a great affection for Rashi, and imparted to him all his own learning. Not to fall behind Maimonides in courtesy, Rashi showed him his commentaries, and Maimonides at the end of his life declared that he would have written more commentaries, had he not been anticipated by the French rabbi.

While in the Orient Rashi is represented as having met a monk, and the two discussed the superiority of their respective religions. At the inn the monk suddenly fell sick. Rashi, caring for him as for a brother, succeeded in curing him by means of a miraculous remedy. The monk wanted to thank him, but Rashi interrupted, saying: "Thou owest me nothing in return. Divided as we are by our religions, we are united by charity, which my religion imposes upon me as a duty. If thou comest upon a Jew in misfortune, aid him as I have aided thee." Fictitious though the story be, it is not unworthy the noble character of Rashi. He *was* noble, therefore noble deeds are ascribed to him.

On his return Rashi is said to have passed through Prague, whither his reputation had preceded him. On his entrance into the synagogue, the acclamations of the faithful proved to him the admiration they felt for the young rabbi of only thirty-six years. The pleasure manifested by the Jews irritated Duke Vratislav, who had the famous rabbi arrested, brought before him, and questioned in the presence of his counsellor, the Bishop of Olmütz. The bishop raising his eyes recognized in the prisoner the Jew who had saved his life, and he told the story to the duke. The order was immediately given to set Rashi free; but the people, thinking the Jews lost, had fallen upon the Jewish quarter. Rashi threw himself at the feet of the sovereign, and begged protection for his brethren. Provided with a safe-conduct, Rashi went forth to appease the mob. The Jews in their great joy saluted him as their savior. Tradition adds that the duke conceived great admiration for the Jewish scholar, and made him one of his advisers.

Another, even sweeter reward, awaited him. Rebecca, the daughter of his host, fell in love with him, and, as

Rashi returned the feeling, her father consented to the marriage.

But all this is on the face of it romance. Certain passages in Rashi's works give abundant proof that Rashi never visited either Palestine or Babylonia, and his conception of the geography of the two countries is utterly fantastic. For instance, he believed that the Euphrates flowed from the one land into the other. Moreover, he himself admitted that his ideas concerning them were gathered only from the Bible and the Talmud.[14]

Though Rashi did not let his curiosity carry him to all parts of the globe, he did not confine himself to his birthplace. He went first to Worms and then to Mayence, remaining some length of time in both places. He was moved to the step, not by taste for travel, but by taste for study, in accordance with the custom of his time, by which a student went from school to school in order to complete his knowledge. Of old, it was customary for the workman to make the tour of France for the purpose of perfecting himself in his trade and finding out the different processes of manufacture. Similarly, the student went from city to city, or, remaining in the same place, from school to school, in order to study a different subject under each master according to the manuscripts which the particular master happened to possess, and which he made his pupils copy. So far from being disqualified from entering a school on account of vagabondage, the stranger student was accorded a warm welcome, especially if he was himself a scholar. Strangers found open hospitality in the community, and were sometimes taken in by the master himself. Knowledge and love of knowledge were safe-conducts. In every city the lettered new-comer found hosts and friends.

Rashi probably stood in need of such hospitality and protection, for, if an obscure remark made by him may be relied upon, his life as a student was not free from care, and he must have suffered all sorts of privations. Nor was it rare that fortune failed to smile upon the students, and—not to give a list of examples—cases of poverty were fairly frequent in the Christian universities, at which mendicancy itself was almost respectable. The temptation might be legitimate to sentimentalize over this love of knowledge, this zeal for work, as they manifested themselves in Rashi, causing him to brave all the evil strokes of fortune for their sake; but one must strain a point to take him literally when he says, as he does in a certain somewhat involved passage, that he studied "without nourishment and without garments." However that may be, the same passage shows that while still a student whose course was but half completed, he married, in conformity with the Talmudic maxim, which recommends the Jew to marry at eighteen years of age. From time to time he went to visit his family at Troyes, always returning to Worms or Mayence.

The fact that the academies of Lorraine which Rashi frequented were in his day the great centres of Talmudic learning, is due to the happy lot which the Jews enjoyed in that country. The chief trading route of Europe at that time connected Italy with Rhenish Germany, and the Jews knew how to render themselves indispensable in the traffic along this route. Moreover, they lived on good terms with their neighbors. The explanation of the

cordial relations between Jews and Christians lies in the
ease with which the Jews rose to the level of general
culture. The architecture of their synagogues is a striking example. The cathedral of Worms was built in 1034,
at the same period as the synagogue there. The two
structures display so many similarities that one is
tempted to believe they represent the handiwork of the
same builders. At all events, it is clear that the Jews
cultivated the Romanesque style, so majestic in its
simplicity.[15]

Lorraine was not at that time a province of the
German Empire; and Rashi leaving the banks of the
Seine for those of the Rhine did not expatriate himself
in the true sense of the word. Lorraine, or, as it was
then called, Lotharingia, the country of Lothair (this is
the name that occurs in the rabbinical sources), was more
than half French. Situated between France and Germany, it came within the sphere of French influence.
French was the language in current use, spoken by Jew
and Christian alike. German words, in fact, were galli-
cized in pronunciation. In Rashi's day the barons of
Lorraine rendered homage to the king of France,
Henry I. Naturally, then, the Jews of Lorraine and
those of Northern France were in close intellectual com-
munion. The academies along the Rhine and the
Moselle formed, as it were, the link between France and
Germany. In general, and despite the rarity and difficulty of communication, the Jews of France, Germany,
and Italy entered freely into relations with one another.[16]

No testimony exists to prove that Rashi, as has been
said, studied at Speyer, at which, without doubt, R.
Eliakim had not yet begun to teach. Possibly, Rashi

did go to Germany, if confidence is to be placed in some information he gives concerning "the country of Ashkenaz," and if the fact may be deduced from the occurrence in his commentaries of some dozen German words, the authenticity of which is not always certain.

Though doubt may attach to Rashi's journeys, it is certain that Rashi passed the larger number of his years of study (about 1055–1065) in Worms. For a long time it was thought—and the belief still obtains—that he also gave instruction in Worms; and recently a street in the city was named after him. Tradition has connected many things with this alleged stay of Rashi as rabbi at Worms. Even in our days visitors are shown the school and the little synagogue attached to it as recalling his sojourn in the place; and a small building touching the eastern wall of the great synagogue is also supposed to perpetuate his memory, and it is still called the "Rashi Chapel." At the bottom of the wall a recess is visible, miraculously caused in order to save his mother when her life was endangered by the two carriages.[17] Some say that Rashi taught from this niche, and a seat in it, raised on three steps, called the Rashi Chair, is still pointed out.

These traditions do not merit credence. Moreover, they are of comparatively recent origin. For a long time the school bore the name, not of Rashi, but of Eleazar of Worms, and it was not built until the beginning of the thirteenth century. Destroyed in 1615, it was restored in 1720 through the generosity of Loeb Sinzheim, of Vienna, and at present it is the Jewish hospital. Alongside the school was a little chapel, belonging to it, which was destroyed in 1615, restored several years

EXTERIOR AND INTERIOR OF THE RASHI CHAPEL AT WORMS

FROM A DRAWING

later, and finally burned by the French in 1689. The other chapel, the so-called "Rashi Chapel," his Yeshibah (school), is so tiny that it could hardly have held the crowd of hearers who thronged there, as tradition has it, in order to listen to him. Besides, the building did not bear the name of Rashi when in 1623 David Joshua Oppenheim, head of the community, erected the school and adjoining chapel, as a Hebrew inscription in the southern wall of the chapel declares. The chapel having lost its utility was closed in 1760, and from this time on it has been consecrated to the memory of Rashi. It was restored in 1855.

At Worms Rashi first studied under the head of the Talmudic academy there, Jacob ben Yakar, by that time a man well on in years. His age doubtless explains the respect and veneration paid him, to which his disciple gave touching expression. But we know besides how sincere was his piety, his humility, and his spirit of self-denial. One day a Christian delivered several tuns of wine to a Jew of Worms under peculiar conditions. Jacob did not want to decide so complicated and delicate a question, and he fled. Rashi and another disciple pursued and overtook him. Then he authorized the use of the wine.

Once when the community was going to pay its respect to the emperor or the governor, Jacob declined the honor of heading the procession. "I am nothing but a poor man," he said. "Let others bring their money, I can offer only my prayers. Each should give of that which he has." Other characteristics of his are mentioned. Once he and his colleague, Eliezer, surnamed the Great, took an animal they had bought to the slaughter house. There it was found that there was an imperfection in its body; according to Eliezer the imperfection rendered it unfit for eating; according to Jacob it was of no importance. The animal having been divided, Eliezer threw his share away. Then Jacob did the same, saying that he would not eat the meat of an animal when another denied himself the enjoyment of it. Later it is told of Jacob that in his humility he swept the floor of the synagogue with his beard. To cite Rashi himself, "I never protest against the usages in the school of my master, Jacob ben Yakar: I know that he possessed the finest qualities. He considered himself a worm which is trodden underfoot, and he never arrogated to himself the honor—though he would have been justified in so doing—of having introduced any innovation whatsoever."

It seems that Rashi, who spoke of Jacob ben Yakar with the utmost respect, and called him "my old master," studied not only the Talmud but also the Bible under his guidance.

The scholar who desired to obtain a grasp on all the studies, if not in their full content, at least in all their variety, had to devote many years to study at a school, not necessarily the same school, throughout his student years, for since the celebrity of a school depended upon the knowledge and renown of its head, it gained and lost pupils with its master.

Thus, on the death of Jacob ben Yakar, Rashi studied under the guidance of his successor, Isaac ben Eleazar ha-Levi,[18] though not for long, it seems. Wishing in a way to complete the cycle of instruction, he went to Mayence, the centre of great Talmudic activity.

The school here was directed by Isaac ben Judah (about 1050–1080), sometimes called the "Frenchman." Rashi considered Isaac ben Judah his master *par excellence*. In this school were composed the Talmudic commentaries generally attributed to R. Gershom and sometimes cited under the title of "Commentaries of the Scholars of Mayence." Isaac ben Judah—not to be confounded with Isaac ha-Levi, both having been the disciples of Eliezer the Great—was scrupulously pious, and absolutely bound by traditional usage.

Rashi, it thus becomes apparent, was not content to learn from only one master; he attended various schools, as if he had had a prevision of his future task, to sum up and, as it were, concentrate all Talmudic teachings and gather the fruits of the scientific activities of all these academies. Similarly, Judah the Saint, before he became the redactor of the Mishnah, placed himself under a number of learned men, "as if," says Graetz, "he had had a presentiment that one day he would collect the most diverse opinions and put an end to the juridical debates of the Tannaim."

Rashi's intellectual status during these years of study must not be misunderstood. Pupil he doubtless was, but such a one as in course of time entered into discussions with his teachers, and to whom questions were submitted for decision. It may even be that toward the end of his school period, he commenced to compose his Talmudic commentaries, or, rather revise the notes of his masters.

At Worms as at Mayence, his fellow-students probably counted among their number those young scholars who remained his friends and correspondents. Such were

Azriel ben Nathan, his kinsman Eliakim ha-Levi ben
Meshullam, of Speyer (born about 1030), Solomon ben
Simson, Nathan ben Machir and his brother Menahem
and Yakar, Meïr ha-Cohen and his son Abraham,
Samuel ha-Levi and, chief of all, his brother David,
Nathan ben Jehiel and his brothers Daniel and Abraham, Joseph ben Judah, Ezra Durbal, and Meïr ben
Isaac ben Samuel[19] (about 1060), acting rabbi and
liturgical poet, mentioned by Rashi in terms of praise
and several times cited by him as an authority. Meïr
of Rameru, later the son-in-law of Rashi, also studied at
the academies of Lorraine, though probably not at the
same time as Rashi, but a short while after.

As is natural, it was of his teachers that Rashi preserved the most faithful recollections, and he refers to
them as authoritative even after he had surpassed them
in knowledge and reputation. He does not always mention their names in repeating their opinions. If it
were possible to make a distinction and decide the
authorship of each sentence, it would be found that we
are not far from the truth in asserting that the greater
part of the pupil's work was the work of his masters.[20]

But in literature, as elsewhere, honor does not redound
to the workmen who have gotten the material together,
but to the architect, wise and skilful, who conceives and
carries out the plan for the entire edifice, and, with the
stones others have brought, constructs a monument of
vast proportions.

CHAPTER III

RASHI AT TROYES—LAST YEARS

The youth Rashi has now completed his apprenticeship; in his studies and travels he has amassed a vast store of information, which he will use for the profit of his contemporaries and of posterity; and he now believes himself in possession of sufficient knowledge and experience to strike out for himself. Moreover, he must now provide for his family—we have seen that he married while still a student. But he does not give up his studies.

His change of abode was the only change in his life, a life of remarkable unity, the life of a student. Rashi gave himself up entirely to study, to study without cessation, and to teaching; but teaching is only a form of pursuing one's studies and summing them up.

I

Detailed and comprehensive though the Talmudic studies were, nevertheless the student, especially if he was gifted, completed the course when he was not much more than twenty years of age. Rashi, then, was probably close to twenty-five years old when he returned from Mayence. This return marks an epoch in the history of rabbinical literature. From that time, the study of the Talmud was cultivated not alone upon the banks of the Rhine, but also in Champagne, which came to rival and

soon supplant Lorraine, and having freed itself from the
subjection of the Rhenish schools, radiated the light of
science. Jews from all over Christian Europe gathered
there to bask in the warmth of the new home of Jewish
learning. Less than ten centuries earlier, the same thing
had happened when Rab transplanted the teaching of the
Law from Palestine to Babylonia, and founded an
academy at Sura, which, for a while rivalling the Palestinian schools, soon eclipsed them, and finally became the
principal centre of Jewish science. The Kabbalist was
not so very far from the truth when he believed that the
soul of Rab had passed into the body of Rashi.

It is noteworthy that this upgrowth of Talmudic
schools in Champagne coincides with the literary movement then beginning in Christian France. In emerging
from the barbarous state of the early middle ages, it
seems that the same breath of life quickened the two
worlds. The city of Troyes played an especially important rôle in matters intellectual and religious. A number
of large councils were held there, and the ecclesiastical
school of Troyes enjoyed a brilliant reputation, having
trained scholars such as Olbert, Pierre Comestor, Pierre
de Celle, and William of the White Hands. And it was
near Troyes that the mighty voices of Abelard and Saint
Bernard resounded.

There is a curious reminder of Rashi's sojourn at
Troyes. As late as 1840 an ancient butcher shop was
still standing, into which, it was remarked, flies never
entered. Jewish tradition has it that the shop was built
on the spot previously occupied by Rashi's dwelling—
hence its miraculous immunity. The same legend is
found among the Christians, but they ascribe the free-

dom from flies to the protection of Saint Loup, the patron saint of the city, who himself worked the miracle. Rashi is linked with Troyes in ways more natural as well. As I have said, certain expressions occur in his works which he himself says refer to his city. Some scholars have even stated that they recognized in the language he used the dialect of Troyes, a variety of the speech of Champagne, itself a French patois.

It is probable that Rashi—who was never at the head of the Talmudic schools of Worms or Prague, as the legends go—exercised the functions of a rabbi at Troyes, that he never kept himself exclusively within the confines of his school, and that he felt it his duty to instruct all his fellow-Jews. In conjunction with his intellectual endowments, he possessed faith and charity, the true sources of strength in religious leadership. He was the natural champion of the weak,[21] the judge and supervisor of all acts. He pronounced judgment in cases more or less distantly connected with religion, that is, in nearly all cases at a period so thoroughly religious in character. Either because he had been appointed their rabbi by the faithful, or because he enjoyed great prestige, Rashi was the veritable spiritual chief of the community, and even exercised influence upon the surrounding communities. The man to preside over the religious affairs of the Jews was chosen not so much for his birth and breeding as for his scholarship and piety, since the rabbi was expected to distinguish himself both in learning and in character. "He who is learned, gentle, and modest," says the Talmud, "and who is beloved of men, he should be judge in his city." As will soon be made clear, Rashi fulfilled this ideal. His piety and amia-

bility, in as great a degree as his learning, won for him
the admiration of his contemporaries and of posterity.
At Troyes there was no room for another at the head of
the community.

Like most of the rabbis of the time, Rashi accepted no
compensation from the community for his services, and
he probably lived from what he earned by viticulture.
Once he begs a correspondent to excuse the shortness of
his letter, because he and his family were busy with the
vintage. "All the Jews," he said, "are at this moment
engaged in the vineyards." In a letter to his son-in-law
Meïr, he gives a description of the wine-presses of Troyes,
in the installation of which a change had been made.
It was deemed fitting that the scholar should provide for
the needs of his family; the law in fact imposed it upon
him as a duty. "Religious study not accompanied by
work of the hands is barren and leads to sin." The
functions of a rabbi were purely honorific in character,
dignifying, and unrelated in kind to mercantile goods,
for which one receives pay. It was forbidden to make the
law a means of earning one's living or a title to glory.
"He who profits by his studies or who studies for his own
interest, compromises his salvation."

When the religious representative showed such devotion and disinterestedness, the pious willingly submitted
themselves to his authority. The spiritual heads of the
communities had as great ascendency over believing Jews
as a king had over his subjects; they were sovereigns in
the realm of the spirit. And Rashi in his time, because
of his learning and piety, exercised the most undisputed
authority. His influence though not so great was comparable, in the sphere in which it could be exercised,

with that of the great Saint Bernard upon the entire
Christian world, or with that of Maimonides upon Judaism in the Arabic countries.

People in all circumstances and from all the surrounding countries addressed themselves to him; and to
the list of his correspondents in Lorraine may be added
the names of several French rabbis, the "wise men" of
Auxerre, the scholar Solomon of Tours, whom Rashi
calls his dear friend, his kinsman Eleazar, and R.
Aaron the Elder. His correspondence on learned
questions was so large that sometimes, as when he was
ill, for instance, he would have his disciples or relatives
help him out with it.[22]

About 1070 Rashi founded a school at Troyes, which
soon became the centre of instruction in the Talmud
for the whole region. As we have seen, Gershom trained
a number of disciples who directed schools, each of
which pursued a particular course. Rashi united
these various tendencies, as later, his work put an
end to the activity of the commentators of the Talmud. An explanation is thus afforded of the legend
repeated by Basnage in these words: "He made a collection of the difficulties he had heard decided during
his travels. On his return to Europe he went to all the
academies and disputed with the professors about the
questions which they were discussing; then he threw to
the floor a page of his collections, which gave a solution
of the problem, and so ended the controversy, without,
however, mentioning the name of the author of the decision. It is alleged that these leaves scattered in
thousands of places were gathered together, and that
from them was composed the commentary on the Tal-

mud." The legend attests Rashi's great reputation.
While he was still quite young, his renown had rapidly
spread.

When in Lorraine, he had from time to time paid a
visit to Troyes, and so, later, when definitely established
in Champagne, he maintained relations with his masters,
especially with Isaac ha-Levi, whom he visited and with
whom he corresponded in the interim of his visits.
Isaac ha-Levi was no less fond of his favorite pupil, and
he inquired of travellers about him. He addressed Responsa to Rashi on questions of Talmudic jurisprudence.
In fact, Rashi continued to solicit advice from his
teachers and keep himself informed of everything concerning schools and Talmudic instruction. In this way
he once learned that a Talmudic scholar of Rome, R.
Kalonymos (ben Sabbataï, born before 1030) had come
after the death of Jacob ben Yakar to establish himself
at Worms, where he died, probably a martyr's death,
during the First Crusade. Kalonymos, who enjoyed a
great reputation, wrote Talmudic commentaries and
liturgical poems. His was a personality rare in that
period.

Rashi's masters, in turn, often applied to their pupil
for advice, choosing him as arbiter and consulting him
with a deference more fitting toward a colleague than
a disciple. Isaac ha-Levi wrote the following words,
in which one detects real esteem and admiration under-
lying epistolary emphasis and the usual exaggeration of
a compliment: "Blessed be the Lord who willed that
this century should not be orphaned, who has steadied
our tottering generation by eminent teachers, such as my
dear and respected friend, my kinsman R. Solomon.

May Israel boast many another such as he!" Equally sincere seems the salutation of a letter written to Rashi by Isaac ben Judah: "To him who is beloved in heaven and honored on earth, who possesses the treasures of the Law, who knows how to resolve the most subtle and profound questions, whose knowledge moves mountains and shatters rocks, etc."

After the death of Rashi's teachers (about 1075) his school assumed even more importance. It eclipsed the academies of Lorraine, and from all the neighboring countries it attracted pupils, who later went forth and spread the teachings of their master abroad. Rashi came to be considered almost the regenerator of Talmudic studies, and in the following generation Eliezer ben Nathan said with pious admiration: "His lips were the seat of wisdom, and thanks to him the Law, which he examined and interpreted, has come to life again."

In this school, justly renowned as the centre of Jewish science, master and pupil were animated by equal love for their work. Entire days were spent there in study, and often, especially in winter, entire nights as well. The studies were regulated by a judicious method. The teacher began to explain a treatise of the Talmud on the first of the month, in order that the students might take their measures accordingly, and not delay coming until after the treatise had been begun. The pupils took notes dictated by the teacher, and thus composed manuscripts which are still of great value. In so doing they fixed all the minutiae of a detailed process of argumentation. On the other hand, books were rare, and students poor. The master himself, in order to facilitate his task, wrote explanations during the lesson, and these served as text-books, which, like the students' notebooks, became treasure houses for later generations.

Rashi not only imparted knowledge to his pupils, but received knowledge from them in turn. He set great store by their observations. His grandson Samuel ben Meïr once drew his attention to a certain form of Biblical parallelism, in which the second hemistich completes the first, as in the following verse from Psalm xciii:

"The floods have lifted up, O Lord,
  The floods have lifted up their voice."

After this, each time Rashi came across a similarly constructed verse, he would say with mock gravity: "Here's a verse for my Samuel."

The Jewish student led a pure, regulated existence, with only wholesome distractions, such as the little celebrations when the study of a Talmudic treatise had been completed. His greatest pleasure he found in the sword-play of mind against mind, in the love of knowledge and religion.

Rashi did not content himself with giving instruction only to students under his immediate influence. He desired that his teachings should not be lost to men unknown to him and to unborn generations. He realized that everything so far accomplished in the field of Talmudic and even Biblical exegesis was inadequate, and he therefore undertook the works that were to occupy him the rest of his life. His school was, so to speak, the laboratory of which his Biblical and Talmudic commentaries were the products. They involved a vast amount of toil, and though death overtook him before his task was accomplished, he doubtless began the work early in life.* A legend goes that he was forbidden to write commentaries on the Bible before he was a hundred years old. Rashi with all his ardor for learning could not curb himself and postpone his activity for so long a time, and he turned the prohibition in his own favor by explaining that the sum of the Hebrew letters forming the word " hundred " amounted to forty-six.

Rashi's disciples were in very truth his sons, for no sons were born to the illustrious rabbi. But he had three daughters, who each married a Talmudist, so that Rashi's descendants, no less than himself, were the bearers of rabbinic learning in France. Rashi did not limit his association with his pupils to the school-house, but invited them to enter his family circle. Indeed, this was the highest honor to which they could aspire. It has always been the greatest piece of good fortune for a Jew to marry the daughter of a learned and pious man, and the suitors most desired by and for young girls were scholars. In this way arose veritable dynasties of rabbis, who cherished learning as a heritage, a family treasure, and the Rashi " dynasty " was one of the greatest and most renowned among them.

Tradition has delighted in representing Rashi's daughters as highly endowed. Unfortunately, it seems that the education of women among the Jews of the middle ages was greatly neglected, though they were taught the principles of religion and the ordinances which it was their special duty to fulfil. They possessed the domestic virtues, and above all modesty and charity. They helped their husbands in business, thus enabling them to devote themselves more freely to study, and though the women themselves lacked learning, they con-

cerned themselves with the learning of their men-folk,
and were eager to contribute to the support of schools
and pupils. They were extremely pious, often scrupulously so. The women in a family of scholars had sufficient knowledge to be called upon in ritual questions,
as, for instance, Bellette, sister of Isaac ben Menahem
the Great, of Orleans, a contemporary of Rashi, who
appealed to her authority. Other cases of the same kind
are mentioned, some occurring in Rashi's own family,
his granddaughter Miriam having been asked to adjudi-
cate a doubtful case. One of Rashi's daughters, also
called Miriam, married the scholar Judah ben Nathan.
Rachel, another daughter, given a French epithet,
Bellassez,[24] also seems to have been learned. Her union
with a certain Eliezer, or Jocelyn, was unhappy. Not so
the marriage of the third daughter of Rashi, Jochebed,
whose husband was the scholar Meïr, son of Samuel, of
Rameru, a little village near Troyes. She had four
sons, named Samuel, Jacob, Isaac, and Solomon. The
three first, and in a less degree the fourth, too, continued
in glorious wise the traditions of their grandfather. I
shall have occasion again to mention them, their life,
and their work.

The renown of his posterity, far from dimming
Rashi's brilliance, only added fresh lustre to the name
of him who was both father and revered master. Even
in his life-time Rashi could reap the harvest of his efforts, and though death intervened before his work was
completed, he saw at his side collaborators ready to continue what he had begun.

A marriage among the Jews of France of that epoch
must have been a charming and touching ceremony, to

judge from a picturesque description, given by an author of the fourteenth century, of a wedding at Mayence, a city in which the community had preserved ancient customs.

Several days before the ceremony the beadle invited all the faithful; for it was a public festival, and everybody was supposed to share in the joy of the bride and bridegroom. On the day of the wedding, the bridegroom, attended by the rabbi and men of standing in the community and followed by other members of the congregation, proceeded to the synagogue to the accompaniment of music. At the synagogue he was awaited by the bride, who was surrounded by her maids of honor and by a number of women. The rabbi presented the young girl to the bridegroom, and he took her hand, while the by-standers showered grains of wheat upon them and small pieces of money, which were picked up by the poor. Then, hand in hand, the couple walked to the door of the synagogue, where they paused a while. After this the bride was led to her own home so that she might complete her toilet. Under a large mantle of silk and fur, with puffed sleeves, she wore a white robe, symbol of the mourning for Zion, the memory of which was not to leave her even on this day of joy. The sign of mourning adopted for the bridegroom was a special headgear.

After the bridegroom had returned to the synagogue and placed himself near the Ark of the Law, the morning service was held. Meanwhile the bride was led to the door of the synagogue, always to the accompaniment of music, and the bridegroom, conducted by the rabbi and the heads of the community, went to receive her there,

He placed himself on her left, and preceded by his mother and the mother of the bride, he guided her to the pulpit in the centre of the synagogue. Here was pronounced the nuptial benediction.

The ceremony over, the husband hastened to his home to meet his wife and introduce her to the dwelling of which she was to be the mistress. Here it was that the wedding feast was spread. Festivities continued for several days, and the following Saturday special hymns were inserted in the service in honor of the newly-wedded couple.[25] No parade or pomp marred the beauty and grace of this ceremony, every act of which bespoke pure poetry and religion.

From this it is evident how much domestic virtues were prized among the Jews of the middle ages. The family was expected to be a model of union and harmony, of tenderness of mate toward mate and parents toward children. Gentleness and a spirit of trust were to preside over the household. Rashi, as we shall see,[26] speaks in moving terms of the high regard which a man owes his wife.

II

But it was not given to Rashi to pass untroubled through his fruitful life of study. A terrible shock surprised him. The eleventh century set in a sea of blood.

Some legends have a hardy life. Not the least remarkable of these is the myth that the Crusades were wholly inspired by religious zeal. These great European movements are always represented as having been called forth by enthusiasm and thirst for self-sacrifice. A great wave of faith, we are told, swept over the masses, and carried them on to the conquest of the Holy Sepulchre. There is another side to the shield—faith fawning on political expediency and egoism, and turning brigand. Without doubt many Christians went on the Crusades impelled by religious conviction. But how many nourished less vague ideas in their hearts? Not to mention those whose only aim was to escape from the consequences of their misdeeds and obtain absolution and indulgences, not to mention those who were animated by a foolish sense of chivalry, by love of adventure, of perilous risks, drawn by the attraction of the unknown and the marvellous—apart from these, there was the great mass, impelled by greed and thirst for pillage.

Complaisant historians express their admiring wonder at these "hundreds of thousands of men fighting with their eyes doggedly fixed upon the Holy Sepulchre and dying in order to conquer it." They pity these "multitudes of men who threw themselves on Islam the unknown, these naïve, trusting spirits, who each day imagined themselves at Jerusalem, and died on the road thither." Would it not be well for them to reserve a little of their admiration and pity for the unfortunates that were the victims of these "naïve" multitudes? Ought they not to say that this religious fervor was a mixture chiefly of blind hate and bloody fanaticism? After a victory the Crusaders would massacre the populations of the conquered cities, including in the slaughter not only the Mohammedans but also the Oriental Christians. Then why should we wonder if on the road to Palestine they laid violent hands on the Jews they found by the way? [27]

It is known what an important part France played in the First Crusade. From France issued the spark that set the entire Occident aflame, and France furnished the largest contingent to the Crusades.

However, the disorders in France were merely local. If the rage for blood enkindled by the First Crusade scarcely affected the Jews of France, it is because the population was concentrated on the banks of the Rhine. But here its murderous frenzy knew no bounds. The people threw themselves on the Jewish communities of Treves, Speyer, Worms, Mayence, and Cologne, and put to death all who refused to be converted (May to July, 1096). The noise of events such as these perforce " found a path through the sad hearts " of the Jews of Champagne; for they maintained lively and cordial relations with their brethren in the Rhine lands, many being bound to them by ties of kinship. Among the martyrs of 1096 was Asher ha-Levi, who was the disciple of Isaac ben Eleazar, Rashi's second teacher, and who died together with his mother, his two brothers, and their families. From a Hebrew text we learn that the Jews of France ordered a fast and prayers in commemoration of these awful massacres, the victims of which numbered not less than ten thousand.

But all could not sacrifice their lives for the sake of their faith. Though so large a number were slain by the pious hordes or slew one another in order to escape violence, others allowed themselves to be baptized, or adopted Christianity, in appearance at least. After the Crusaders were at a distance, on the way to their death in the Orient, the Jews left behind could again breathe freely. Of many of them, Gregory of Tours might have said that " the holy water had washed their bodies but not their hearts, and, liars toward God, they returned to their original heresy." The emperor of Germany, Henry IV, it seems, even authorized those who had been forced into baptism to return to Judaism, and the baptized Jews hastened to throw off the hateful mask. This benevolent measure irritated the Christian clergy, and the Pope bitterly reproached the Emperor.

What sadder, more curious spectacle than that which followed? Many of those Jews who had remained faithful to their religion would not consider the apostates as their brethren, unwilling apostates though they had been, and strenuously opposed their re-admission to the Synagogue.

This unwillingness to compound, showing so little generosity and charity, must have distressed Rashi profoundly. For, when consulted in regard to the repulsed converts, he displayed a loftiness of view and a breadth of tolerance which Maimonides himself could not equal. In similar circumstances Maimonides, it seems, in intervening, yielded a little to personal prepossession. " Let us beware," wrote Rashi, " let us beware of alienating those who have returned to us by repulsing them. They became Christians only through fear of death; and as soon as the danger disappeared, they hastened to return to their faith."

Though the First Crusade affected the Jews of France only indirectly, it none the less marks a definite epoch in their history. The fanaticism it engendered wreaked its fury upon the Jews, against whom all sorts of odious charges were brought. They were placed in the same category as sorcerers and lepers, and among the crimes laid at their door were ritual murder and piercing of the host. The instigations of the clergy did not remain without effect upon a people lulled to sleep by its ignorance, but aroused to action by its faith. The kings and seigneurs on their side exploited the Jews, and expelled them from their territories.

Rashi had the good fortune not to know these troublous times. But he discerned in a sky already overcast the threatening premonitions of a tempest, and as though to guard his fellow-Jews against the danger, he left them a work which was to be a viaticum and an asylum to them. When one sees how Rashi's work brought nourishment, so to speak, to all later Jewish literature, which was a large factor in keeping Israel from its threatened ruin, one is convinced that Rashi, aside from his literary efforts, contributed no slight amount toward the preservation and the vitality of the Jewish people.

Even if the Crusades had not involved persecution of the Jews and so provoked the noble intervention of Rashi, they would nevertheless have made themselves felt in Champagne. Count Hugo, among others, remained in the Holy Land from 1104 to 1108; and his brother was killed at Ramleh in 1102. According to a rather wide-spread legend, Rashi stood in intimate relations with one of the principal chiefs of the Crusade, the famous duke of Lower Lotharingia, Godfrey of Bouillon. Historians have found that the part actually played by the duke in the Crusades is smaller than that ascribed to him by tradition, yet the profound impression he made on the popular imagination has remained, and legend soon endowed him with a fabulous genealogy, making of him an almost mythical personage. A favorite trick of the makers of legends is to connect their heroes with celebrated contemporaries, as though brilliance was reflected from one upon the other. Thus Saladin was connected with Maimonides and with Richard the Lion-Hearted, and, similarly, Rashi with Godfrey of Bouillon.

The story goes that Godfrey, having heard rumors of the knowledge and wisdom of the rabbi of Troyes, summoned Rashi to his presence to consult with him upon the issue of his undertaking. Rashi refused to appear. Annoyed, Godfrey accompanied by his cavaliers went to the rabbi's school. He found the door open, but the great building empty. By the strength of his magic Rashi had made himself invisible, but he himself could see everything. "Where art thou, Solomon?" cried the cavalier. "Here I am," a voice answered; "what does my lord demand?" Godfrey not seeing a living soul repeated his question, and always received the same answer. But not a man to be seen! Utterly confounded, he left the building and met a disciple of Rashi's. "Go tell thy master," he said, "that he should appear; I swear he has nothing to fear from me." The rabbi then revealed himself.[28] "I see," Godfrey said to him, "that thy wisdom is great. I should like to know whether I shall return from my expedition victorious, or whether I shall succumb. Speak without fear."

"Thou wilt take the Holy City," Rashi replied, "and thou wilt reign over Jerusalem three days, but on the fourth day the Moslem will put thee to flight, and when thou returnest only three horses will be left to thee."

"It may be," replied Godfrey, irritated and disillusioned in seeing his future pictured in colors so sombre. "But if I return with only one more horse than thou sayest, I shall wreak frightful vengeance upon thee. I shall throw thy body to the dogs, and I shall put to death all the Jews of France."

After several years of fighting Godfrey of Bouillon, ephemeral king of Jerusalem, took his homeward road back to France, accompanied by three cavaliers, in all, then, four horses, one more than Rashi had predicted. Godfrey remembered the rabbi's prophecy, and determined to carry out his threat. But when he entered the city of Troyes, a large rock, loosened from the gate, fell upon one of the riders, killing him and his horse. Amazed at the miracle, the duke perforce had to recognize that Rashi had not been wrong, and he wanted to go to the seer to render him homage, but he learned that Rashi had died meanwhile. This grieved him greatly.

This legend was further embellished by the addition of details. Some placed the scene at Worms; others asserted that the duke asked Rashi to accompany him to Lorraine; but Rashi nobly refused, as Maimonides did later. All forgot that Godfrey of Bouillon after he left for the Crusades never saw his fatherland again, but died at Jerusalem, five years before Rashi.

Rashi's life offers no more noteworthy events. He passed the balance of his days in study, in guiding the community, and in composing his works. Without doubt, our lack of information concerning his last years is due to this very fact—to the peace and calm in which that time was spent.

A naïve legend has it that he wanted to know who would be his companion in Paradise. He learned in a dream that the man lived at Barcelona, and was called Abraham the Just. In order to become acquainted with him while still on earth, Rashi, despite his great age, started forth on a journey to Barcelona. There he found a very rich man, but, as was alleged, he was also very impious. However, Rashi was not long in discovering that for all his life of luxury he was just and generous of spirit. Rashi even composed a work in his honor entitled "The Amphitryon," in Hebrew, *Ha-Parnas*. Do you think the work was lost? Not a bit of it. It still exists, but it is called *Ha-Pardes*. The legend is based upon a copyist's mistake. However, it is found in different forms in other literatures.

Beyond a doubt Rashi died and was buried in his birthplace. Nevertheless the story is told, that as he was about to return to France with his young wife, the daughter of his host at Prague, after his long trip of study and exploration, which I have already described, an unknown man entered his dwelling and struck him a mortal blow. But the people could not resign themselves to accept so miserable an end for so illustrious a man, and the legend received an addition. At the very moment Rashi was to be buried, his wife ran up and brought him back to life by means of a philtre. His father-in-law, in order not to excite the envy of his enemies, kept the happy event a secret, and ordered the funeral to be held. The coffin was carried with great pomp to the grave, which became an object of veneration for the Jews of Prague. In fact, a tomb is pointed out as being that of the celebrated rabbi. and, as the inscription is effaced, the assertion can safely be made that Rashi died in the capital of Bohemia.

Rashi's death was less touching and less tragic. We learn from a manuscript dated Thursday, the twenty-ninth of Tammuz, in the year 4865 of the Creation (July 13, 1105), that Rashi died at Troyes. He was then sixty-five years of age.

It is as though the echo of the regrets caused by Rashi's death resounded in the following note in an old manuscript: " As the owner of a fig-tree knows when it is time to cull the figs, so God knew the appointed time of Rashi, and carried him away in his hour to let him enter heaven. Alas! he is no more, for God has taken him." These few lines, without doubt the note of some copyist, show with what deep respect the memory of Rashi came to be cherished but shortly after his death. Like Rabbenu Gershom he was awarded after his death the title of " Light of the Captivity." But later the title was applied only to Gershom, as though Rashi had no need of it to distinguish him.

Rashi died " full of days," having led a life of few incidents, because it was uniformly devoted to study and labor. He was like a patriarch who is surrounded by the affection of his children and by the respect of his contemporaries. To future generations he bequeathed the memory of his virtues and the greatness of his work. And his memory has survived the neglect of time and the ingratitude of man. Posterity has enveloped his brow with a halo of glory, and after the lapse of eight centuries the radiance of his personality remains un-diminished.

CHAPTER IV

Character and Learning of Rashi

Not only is there little information concerning the incidents of Rashi's life, but also there are only a few sources from which we can learn about his mental make-up and introduce ourselves, so to speak, into the circle of his thoughts and ideas. Generally one must seek the man in his work. But into writings so objective as those of a commentator who does not even exert himself to set forth his method and principles in a preface, a man is not apt to put much of his own personality. Moreover, Rashi was disposed to speak of himself as little as possible. From time to time, however, he lets a confidence escape, and we treasure it the more carefully because of its rarity.

Fortunately we can get to know him a little better through his letters, that is, through the Responsa addressed by him to those who consulted him upon questions of religious law. Another source, no less precious, is afforded by the works of his pupils, who noted with pious care the least acts or expressions of their master that were concerned with points of law.

I shall endeavor to sum up all this information, so that we may get a picture of the man and trace his features in as distinct lines as possible.

I

Needless to say, Rashi's conduct was always honorable and his manners irreproachable. To be virtuous was not to possess some special merit; it was the strict fulfilment of the Law. We have seen that Rashi's life was pure; and his life and more particularly his work reveal a firm, controlled nature, a simple, frank character, clear judgment, upright intentions, penetrating intelligence, and profound good sense. The Talmudic maxim might be applied to him: "Study demands a mind as serene as a sky without clouds." His was a questioning spirit, ever alert. He had the special gift of viewing the outer world intelligently and fixing his attention upon the particular object or the particular circumstance that might throw light upon a fact or a text. For instance, although he did not know Arabic, he remembered certain groups of related words in the language, which had either been called to his attention or which he had met with in reading. He noticed of his own accord that "Arabic words begin with 'al'." To give another example of this discernment: he explains a passage of the Talmud by recalling that he saw Jews from Palestine beating time to mark the melody when they were reading the Pentateuch.

The clearness and poise of Rashi's intellect—qualities which he possessed in common with other French rabbis, though in a higher degree—stand in favorable contrast with the sickly symbolism, the unwholesome search for mystery, which tormented the souls of ecclesiastics, from the monk Raoul Glaber up to the great Saint Bernard, that man, said Michelet, "diseased by the love of God."

Yet the Jews of Northern France were not, as one might suppose from their literature, cold and dry of temperament. They were sensitive and tender-hearted. They did not forever lead the austere life of scholarly seclusion; they did not ignore the affections nor the cares of family; they knew how to look upon life and its daily come and go.

But they did not go to the other extreme and become philosophers. Traditional religion was to them the entire truth. They never dreamed that antagonism might arise between faith and reason. From a theological point of view—if the modern term may be employed—Rashi shared the ideas of his time. In knowledge or character one may raise oneself above one's contemporaries; but it is rare not to share their beliefs and superstitions. Now, it must be admitted, the Jews of Northern France did not cherish religion in all its ideal purity. The effect of their faith, their piety, upon these simple souls was to make them somewhat childish, and give their practices a somewhat superstitious tinge. Thus, Rashi says in the name of his teacher Jacob ben Yakar, that one should smell spices Saturday evening, because hell, after having its work interrupted by the Sabbath, begins to exhale a bad odor again in the evening. This naïve faith at least preserved Rashi from pursuing the paths not always avoided by his co-religionists of Spain and the Provence, who dabbled in philosophy. Rashi never was conscious of the need to justify certain narratives or certain beliefs which shocked some readers of the Bible. Not until he came upon a passage in the Talmud which awakened his doubts did he feel called upon to explain why God created humanity, though He knew it would become corrupt, and why He asks for information concerning things which cannot escape His omniscience. But Rashi was not bewildered by certain anthropomorphic passages in the Bible, the meaning of which so early a work as the Targum had veiled. Nor was he shocked by the fact that God let other peoples adore the stars, and that altars had been consecrated to Him elsewhere than at Jerusalem. Thus his plain common sense kept him from wandering along by-paths and losing himself in the subtleties in which the Ibn Ezras and the Nahmanides were entangled. His common sense rendered him the same service in the interpretation of many a Talmudic passage that Saadia and Nissim had thought incapable of explanation unless wrested from its literal meaning. Since justice requires the admission, I shall presently dwell upon the points in which Rashi's lack of philosophic training was injurious to him. Here it is necessary merely to note wherein it was useful to him. It was not he, for instance, who held Abraham and Moses to have been the precursors—no, the disciples—of Aristotle. Ought we to complain of that?

In discussing the fundamental goodness of Rashi's nature, no reserves nor qualifications need be made. Historians have vied with one another in praising his humanity, his kindliness, his indulgent, charitable spirit, his sweetness, and his benevolence. He appealed to the spirit of concord, and exhorted the communities to live in peace with one another. His goodness appears in the following Responsum to a question, which the interrogator did not sign: "I recognized the author of the letter by the writing. He feared to sign his name, because he suspects me of being hostile to him. But I assure him I am not; I have quite the contrary feeling for him." A still quainter characteristic is illustrated by the following decision which he rendered: "If, during the prayer after a meal, one interrupts oneself to feed an animal, one does not commit a reprehensible act, for one should feed one's beasts before taking nourishment, as it is written: 'And I will send grass in thy fields for thy cattle, that thou mayest eat and be full.'" But the quality Rashi possessed in the highest degree was simplicity, modesty, one may almost say, humility; and what contributed not a little to the even tenor of his existence was his capacity for self-effacement.

Such was his nature even when a youth in the academies of Lorraine. He himself tells how once, when he was in the house of his teacher, he noticed that a ritual prescription was being violated in dressing the meat of a sheep. His teacher, occupied with other matters, did not notice the infringement of the law, and the pupil was in a quandary. To keep quiet was to cover up the wrong and make it irreparable; to speak and pronounce a decision before his master was to be lacking in respect for him. So, to escape from the embarrassing situation, Rashi put a question to his master bearing upon the dressing of the meat.

Toward all his teachers Rashi professed the greatest respect. On a certain question they held wrong opinions, and Rashi wrote: "I am sure they did not cause irremediable harm, but they will do well in the future to abstain from such action." This shows at the same time that Rashi did not hesitate to be independent, did not blindly accept all their teachings. When he believed an opinion wrong, he combated it; when he believed an opinion right, he upheld it, even against his masters. On one occasion, Isaac ha-Levi delivered a sentence which to his pupil seemed too strict. " I plied him with questions," says Rashi, " to which he would not pay attention, although he could not give any proof in support of his opinion." To the pupils of Isaac, he wrote: " I do not pretend to abolish the usages that you follow, but as soon as I can be with you, I shall ask you to come over to my opinion. I do not wish to discuss the stricter practices adopted in the school of Jacob ben Yakar (Isaac's predecessor), until I shall have established that my idea is the correct one. He will then acknowledge that I am right, as he did once before."

This is the circumstance referred to. While still a pupil of Isaac ha-Levi, Rashi had accepted a decision of his without having thoroughly studied it. Later he became convinced that his teacher was mistaken, but he bore it in mind until he went to Worms and persuaded his teacher to his own belief.

Rashi displayed the same reserve in the exercise of his rabbinical functions, especially when the community appealing to him was not that of Troyes. That of Châlons-sur-Saône once consulted him concerning an interdiction imposed by R. Gershom, and asked him to repeal it; but Rashi modestly declined to give an opinion.[20]

Rashi's modesty is also illustrated by the tone of his correspondence. Deferential or indulgent, he never adopted a superior manner, was never positive or dogmatic. When his correspondents were wrong, he sought to justify their mistakes; when he combated the explanation of another, he never used a cutting expression, or a spiteful allusion, as Ibn Ezra did, and so many others.

Finally, it seems, he did not hesitate to recognize his own mistakes, even when a pupil pointed them out to him, and it is possible to select from his commentaries a number of avowals of error. In his Responsa he wrote: "The same question has already been put to me, and I gave a faulty answer. But now I am convinced of my mistake, and I am prepared to give a decision better based on reason. I am grateful to you for having drawn my attention to the question; thanks to you, I now see the truth." This question concerned a point in Talmudic law; but he was willing to make a similar admission in regard to the explanation of a Biblical verse. "In commenting on Ezekiel I made a mistake in the explanation of this passage, and as, at the end of the chapter, I gave the true sense, I contradicted myself. But in taking up the question again with my friend Shemaiah,[30] I hastened to correct this mistake."

An old scholar named R. Dorbal, or Durbal, addressed a question to Rashi, and Rashi in his reply expressed his astonishment that an old man should consult so young a man as he. Assuredly, said Rashi, it was because he wanted to give a proof of his benevolence and take the occasion for congratulating Rashi on his response, if it were correct.

It would take too long to enumerate all the passages in which Rashi avows his ignorance, and declares he cannot give a satisfactory explanation.

We have seen that Rashi did not hesitate to acknowledge that he owed certain information to his friends and
pupils, and that his, debates with them had sometimes led
him to change his opinion.   The confession he made one
day to his grandson Samuel about the inadequacy of his
Biblical Commentary [31] has become celebrated, and justly
so.   There is something touching in the way he listened
to the opinions of his grandson, and accepted them
because they appeared correct to him—the man who
loved truth and science above everything else.   Like
many noble spirits, he considered his work imperfect,
and would have liked to do it all over again.   This
modesty and this realization of the truth are the ruling
qualities of his nature.

II

The ideal Jew combines virtue with knowledge, and
tradition ascribes to Rashi universal knowledge.   In the
first place he was a polyglot.   Popular admiration of
him, based upon the myth concerning his travels and
upon a superficial reading of his works, assigned to him
the old miracle of the Apostles.   The languages he was
supposed to know were Latin, Greek, Arabic, and Persian.   He was also said to be acquainted with astronomy,
and even with the Kabbalah, of which, according to the
Kabbalists, he was an ardent adept.   After his death,
they say, he appeared to his grandson Samuel to teach
him the true pronunciation of the Ineffable Name.
Medical knowledge was also attributed to Rashi, and a
medical work ascribed to his authorship.   One scholar
went so far as to call him a calligrapher.[32]   From his
infancy, it was declared, he astonished the world by his

learning and by his memory; and when, toward the end of his life, he went to Barcelona, he awakened every one's admiration by his varied yet profound knowledge.

These errors, invented, or merely repeated, but, at all events, given credence by the Jewish chroniclers and the Christian bibliographers, cannot hold out against the assaults of criticism. To give only one example of Rashi's geographical knowledge, it will suffice to recall how he represented the configuration of Palestine and Babylonia, or rather how he tried to guess it from the texts.[33] His ignorance of geography is apparent in his commentaries, which contain a rather large number of mistakes. In addition, Rashi was not always familiar with natural products, or with the creations of art, or with the customs and usages of distant countries. Still less was a rabbi of the eleventh century likely to have an idea of what even Maimonides was unacquainted with, the local color and the spirit of dead civilizations. Rashi—to exemplify this ignorance—explained Biblical expressions by customs obtaining in his own day: "to put into possession," the Hebrew of which is "to fill the hand," he thinks he explains by comparing it with a feudal ceremony and discovering in it something analogous to the act of putting on gauntlets. In general, the authors of Rashi's time, paying little regard to historic setting, explained ancient texts by popular legends, or by Christian or feudal customs. Therefore, one need not scruple to point out this defect in Rashi's knowledge. Like his compatriots he did not know the profane branches of learning. He was subject to the same limitations as nearly the entire body of clergy of his day. While the Arabs so eagerly and successfully cultivated philosophy, medicine, astronomy, and physics, Christian Europe was practically ignorant of these sciences. Finally, one will judge still less severely of Rashi's knowledge—or lack of knowledge—if one remembers what science was in the Christian world of the middle ages—it was childish, tinged with superstition, extravagantly absurd, and fantastically naïve. Rashi believed that the Nile flooded its banks once every forty years; but Joinville, who lived two centuries later, and who was in Egypt, tells even more astonishing things than this about the marvellous river, which has its source in the terrestrial Paradise.

Besides French, the only profane language Rashi knew was German. The explanations he gives according to the Greek, the Arabic, and the Persian, he obtains from secondary sources. Indeed, they are sometimes faulty, and they reveal the ignorance of the man who reproduced without comprehending them. No great interest attaches to the mention of his chronological mistakes and his confusion of historical facts. His astronomic knowledge is very slight, and resolves itself into what he borrowed from the Italian Sabbataï Donnolo, of Oria (about 950).

But limited as his knowledge was to Biblical, Talmudic, and Rabbinical literature, it was for that reason all the greater in the province he had explored in its inmost recesses. This is shown by his numerous citations, the sureness of his touch, and his mastery of all the subjects of which he treats.

Thanks to the citations, we can definitely ascertain what we might call his library.

Needless to say, the first place was held by the Bible, which, as will be seen, he knew perfectly. He wrote commentaries upon the Bible almost in its entirety, besides frequently referring to it in his Talmudic commentaries. His favorite guide for the explanation of the Pentateuch is the Aramaic version by Onkelos. For the Prophets he used the Targum of Jonathan ben Uzziel.[34] He was entirely ignorant of the Apocryphal books. The Wisdom of Ben Sira, for instance, like the *Megillat Taanit,* or Roll of Fasts,[35] were known to him only through the citations of the Talmud.

On the other hand Rashi was thoroughly conversant with the whole field of Talmudic literature—first of all the treatises on religious jurisprudence, the *Mishnah,*[36] *Tosefta,*[37] the Babylonian and, in part, the Palestinian *Gemara*[38]; then, the Halakic Midrashim, such as the *Mekilta,* the *Sifra,* the *Sifre,*[38] and Haggadic compilations, such as the *Rabbot,*[39] the Midrash on the Song of Songs, on Lamentations, Ecclesiastes, the Psalms, and Samuel, the *Pesikta,*[40] the *Tanḥuma,*[41] and the *Pirke de Rabbi Eliezer.*[42]

According to tradition, Rashi has set the Talmudic period as the date of composition of two works which modern criticism has placed in the period of the Geonim. These works are the historic chronicle *Seder Olam*[43] and the gnostic or mystic treatise on the Creation, the *Sefer Yezirah,* the forerunner of the Kabbalah. Besides these anonymous works, Rashi knew the Responsa of the Geonim, which he frequently cites, notably those of Sherira[44] and his son Haï,[45] the *Sheeltot* of R. Aḥa,[46] and the *Halakot Gedolot,* attributed by the French school to Yehudaï Gaon.[47] In the same period must be placed two other writers concerning whom we are not wholly enlightened, Eleazar ha-Kalir and the author of the Jewish chronicle entitled *Yosippon*. Eleazar, who lived in the eighth or ninth century, was one of the first liturgical poets both as to time and as to merit. The author of the *Yosippon* undoubtedly lived in Italy in the tenth century. Rashi, like all his contemporaries, confounded the two respectively with the Tanna R. Eleazar and the celebrated Josephus. They were considered authorities by all the rabbis of the middle ages, the first for his language and his Midrashic traditions, the second for his historical knowledge.[48]

So far as the literature contemporary, or nearly contemporary, with Rashi is concerned, it must be stated that Rashi had read all the works written in Hebrew, while the whole of Arabic literature was inaccessible to him. Without doubt he knew the grammarian Judah Ibn Koreish [49] only by the citations from him. On the other hand he made much use of the works of the two Spanish grammarians, Menahem ben Saruk and Dunash ben Labrat,[50] likewise the works of Moses ha-Darshan, of Narbonne. Naturally, he was still better versed in all the rabbinical literature of Northern France and of Germany. He frequently cites R. Gershom, whom he once called "Father and Light of the Captivity," as well as his contemporaries Joseph Tob Elem, Eliezer the Great, and Meshullam ben Kalonymos, of Mayence. I have already mentioned—and will repeat further on— how much he owed his teachers.

For the sake of completeness, it is necessary to add to this list all the contemporaries from whom Rashi learned either directly or indirectly. For information concern-

ing the Talmud, Isaac ben Menahem the Great, of
Orleans, may be mentioned among these; and for infor-
mation concerning the Bible, Menahem ben Helbo, whom
Rashi probably cited through the medium of one of his
pupils or his writings, for he himself was not known to
Rashi, his younger contemporary.

If one also takes into consideration the less important
and the anonymous persons whose books or oral teachings
Rashi cited, one will be convinced that he had what is
called a well-stocked brain, and that his knowledge in
his special domain was as vast as it was profound, since
it embraced the entire field of knowledge which the Jews
of Northern France of that time could possibly cultivate.
His learning was not universal; far from it; but he was
master of all the knowledge his countrymen possessed.

Thanks to this erudition, he could fill, at least in part,
the gaps in his scientific education.   In fact, an understanding of Talmudic law presupposes a certain amount
of information—geometry and botany for questions concerning land, astronomy for the fixation of the calendar,
zoology for dietary laws, and so on.   Rashi's knowledge,
then, was less frequently defective than one is led to
suppose, although sometimes he lagged behind the Talmud itself.   It has been noted that of 127 or 128 French
glosses bearing upon the names of plants, 62 are absolutely correct.   In history Rashi preserved some traditions which we can no longer verify, but which seem to
be derived from sources worthy of confidence; and if it
had not been for Rashi, we would not have become
acquainted with them.

What he knew, therefore, he knew chiefly through
reading and through the instruction of his teachers, to

whom he often appealed; for he possessed that most precious quality in a scholar, conscience, scientific probity. One example will suffice to give an idea of his method. Once, when he was searching for a text in his copy of the Talmud, he found it corrected. But he did not remember if he himself or his teacher had made the correction. So he consulted a manuscript in which he had noted down the variants of his teacher Isaac of Mayence. Not being able to determine from this, he begged his correspondent to look up the manuscript of Isaac and to let him know the reading.

This characteristic leads us back to a consideration of Rashi's nature, upon which one likes to dwell, because it makes him a sage in the most beautiful and the largest meaning of the word, because it makes him one of the most sympathetic personalities in all Jewish history. If Rashi had left nothing but the remembrance of an exemplary life and of spotless virtue, his name would have merited immortality.

But Rashi bequeathed more than this to posterity; he left one, nay, two monuments to awaken admiration and call forth gratitude. They assure him fame based on a solid foundation. What matter if we Jews fail to honor our great men with statues of marble and bronze, if they themselves establish their glory on pedestals that defy the ravages of time? Statues raised by the hand of man are perishable as man himself; the works constructed by a genius are immortal as the genius himself.

BOOK II

THE WORK OF RASHI

BOOK II

The Work of Rashi

CHAPTER V

The Commentaries—General Characteristics

Rashi stands before us a teacher distinguished and original, a religious leader full of tact and delicate feeling, a scholar clear-headed and at the same time loving-hearted. In which capacity, as teacher, religious leader, scholar, does he evoke our deepest admiration? Shall we accord it to the one who made a home for Talmudic studies on the banks of the Seine, and so gave a definite impetus to French Jewish civilization? Or shall we accord it to the one who for nearly forty years presided over the spiritual destinies of an active and studious population and fulfilled the duties of a rabbi; with all the more devotion, without doubt, because he did not have the title of rabbi? Or should we not rather pay our highest tribute to Rashi the man, so upright and modest, so simple and amiable, who has won for himself the veneration of posterity as much by the qualities of his heart as by those of his intellect, as much by his goodness and kindliness as by the subtlety and acumen of his mind, in a word, as much by his character as by his knowledge? Nevertheless his knowledge was extraordinary and productive of great works, which we shall consider in the following chapters.

As spiritual chief of the French Jews, it was natural that Rashi should occupy himself with the source of their intellectual and religious activity, with the Bible. But in his capacity of Talmudist and teacher, it was equally natural that he should devote himself to the explanation of the Talmud, which formed the basis of instruction in the schools, besides serving to regulate the acts of every-day life and the practices of religion. And as a rabbinical authority he was called upon to resolve the problems that arose out of individual difficulties or out of communal questions. We need no other guide than this to lead us to an understanding of his works. But not to omit anything essential, it would be well to mention some collections which were the result of his instruction, and some liturgical poems attributed to him.

*   *   *   *   *   *   *   *

Rashi owes his great reputation to his commentaries on the two great works that comprehend Jewish life in its entirety, and lie at the very root of the intellectual development of Judaism, the Bible and the Talmud. His commentaries involving an enormous amount of labor are all but complete; they fail to cover only a few books of the Bible and a few treatises of the Talmud. The conjecture has been made that at first he set himself to commenting on the Talmud, and then on the Bible, because at the end of his life he expressed the wish that he might begin the Biblical commentary all over again. But this hypothesis is not justified. The unfinished

state of both commentaries, especially the one on the
Talmud, shows that he worked on them at the same time.
But they were not written without interruption, not " in
one spurt," as the college athlete might say. Rashi
worked at them intermittently, going back to them
again and again. It is certain that so far as the Talmudic treatises are concerned, he did not exert himself
to follow the order in which they occur. He may have
taken them up when he explained them in his school.
But in commenting on the Bible, it seems, he adhered
to the sequence of the books, for it was on the later books
that he did not have the time to write commentaries.
Moreover, he sometimes went back to his commentary on
a Biblical book or a Talmudic treatise, not because he
worked to order, like Ibn Ezra, and as circumstances
dictated, but because he was not satisfied with his former
attempt, and because, in the course of his study, the same
subject came up for his consideration. Though the commentaries, then, were not the result of long, steady application, they demanded long-continued efforts, and they
were, one may say, the business of his whole life. The
rabbi Isaac of Vienna, who possessed an autograph commentary of Rashi, speaks of the numerous erasures and
various marks with which it was embroidered.

The commentaries of Rashi, which do not bear special
titles, are not an uninterrupted exposition of the entire
work under consideration, and could not be read from
cover to cover without recourse to the text explained;
they are rather detached glosses, postils, to borrow an
expression from ecclesiastical literature, upon terms or
phrases presenting some difficulties. They are always
preceded by the word or words to be explained.

It is evident, then, that Rashi's works do not bear witness to great originality, or, better, to great creative force. Rashi lacks elevation in his point of view, breadth of outlook, and largeness of conception. He possessed neither literary taste nor esthetic sense. He was satisfied to throw light upon an obscurity, to fill up a lacuna, to justify an apparent imperfection, to explain a peculiarity of style, or to reconcile contradictions. He never tried to call attention to the beauties of the text or to give a higher idea of the original; he never succeeded in bringing into relief the humanity of a law, or the universal bearing of an event.

Rashi failed also to regard a thing in its entirety. He did not write prefaces to his works setting forth the contents of the book and the method to be pursued.[51] In the body of the commentaries, he hardly ever dwells on a subject at length, but contents himself with a brief explanation. In short, his horizon was limited and he lacked perspective. It is to be regretted that he did not know the philosophic works of Saadia, who would have opened up new worlds to him, and would have enlarged the circle of his ideas. If he had read only the Biblical commentaries of the great Gaon, he would have learned from him how to grasp a text in its entirety and give a general idea of a work.

Even if he had limited himself to the Talmud, Rashi, without doubt, would have been incapable of raising a vast and harmonious edifice, like the *Mishneh Torah* of Maimonides. He did not possess the art of developing the various sides of a subject so as to produce a well-ordered whole. He lacked not only literary ambition, but also that genius for organizing and systematizing which classifies and co-ordinates all the laws. Though methodical, he lacked the power to generalize.

This defect, common to his contemporaries, arose, possibly, from a certain timidity. He believed that he ought to efface himself behind his text, and not let his own idea take the place of the author's, especially when the text was a religious law and the author the Divine legislator. But it seems that his power of creative thought was not strong, and could exercise itself only upon the more original works of others. We find analogous features in scholastic literature, which developed wholly in the shadow of the Scriptures, the Fathers of the Church, and Aristotle.

This narrow criticism, this eye for detail, this lack of general ideas and of guiding principles at least guarded Rashi against a danger more original spirits failed to escape, namely, of reading preconceived notions into the text, of interpreting it by an individual method, and, thus, of gathering more meaning, or another meaning, than was intended by the author. Unlike the Jewish and Christian theologians, Rashi felt no need to do violence to the text in order to reconcile it with his scientific and philosophic beliefs.

Though Rashi, as I said, had not a creative intellect, he yet had all the qualities of a commentator. First of all, he possessed clearness, the chief requisite for a commentary, which undertakes to explain a work unintelligible to its readers. "To write like Rashi" has become a proverbial expression for "to write clearly and intelligibly." Rashi always or nearly always uses the expression one expects. He finds the explanation that obtrudes itself because it is simple and easy; he excels in unravelling difficulties and illuminating obscurities. To facilitate comprehension by the reader Rashi resorted to the use of pictures and diagrams, some of which still appear in his Talmudic commentary, though a number have been suppressed by the editors. Once, when asked for the explanation of a difficult passage in Ezekiel, he replied that he had nothing to add to what he had said in his commentary, but he would send a diagram which would render the text more intelligible. It is remarkable with what ease, even without the aid of illustrations, he unravelled the chapters of Ezekiel in which the Prophet describes the Temple of his fancy; or the equally complicated chapters of Exodus which set forth the plan of the Tabernacle.

Essentially this power of exposition is the attribute of intelligent insight. Rashi's was the clearest, the most transparent mind—no clouds nor shadows, no ambiguities, no evasions. He leaves nothing to be taken for granted, he makes no mental reservations. He is clearness and transparency itself.

But Rashi's language is not merely clear; it is extremely precise. It says with accuracy exactly what it sets out to say. Rashi did not hesitate sometimes to coin new words for the sake of conveying his thought. He always heeded the connotation of a word, and took the context into account. Once, in citing a Talmudic explanation of a verse in Jeremiah, he rejected it, because it did not square with the development of the thought; and often he would not accept an interpretation, because a word in the text was given a meaning which it did not have in any other passage. He grasped, and rendered in turn with perfect accuracy, shades of meaning and subtleties of language; and the fine expression of relations difficult to solve surprises and charms the reader by its precision.

Commentators in the effort to be clear are often wordy, and those who aim at brevity often lack perspicuity. The latter applies to Abraham Ibn Ezra, who might have said with the poet, " I avoid long-windedness, and I become obscure." Samuel ben Meïr, on the other hand, grandson and pupil of Rashi, is, at least in his Talmudic commentaries, so long-winded and prolix that at first glance one can detect the additions made by him to the commentaries of his grandfather. It is related, that once, when Rashi was ill, Samuel finished the commentary Rashi had begun, and when Rashi got well he weighed the leaves on which his pupil had written and said: " If thou hadst commented on the whole Talmud after this fashion, thy commentary would have been as heavy as a chariot." The story, which attributes somewhat uncharitable words to Rashi, yet contains an element of truth, and emphasizes the eminent quality of his own commentaries.

He rarely goes into very long explanations. Often he solves a difficulty by one word, by shooting one flash of light into the darkness. The scholar and bibliographer Azulaï scarcely exaggerated when he said that Rashi could express in one letter that for which others needed whole pages. A close study of the Talmudic commentaries shows that he replied in advance and very briefly to the questions of many a Talmudist.

It is only in considering the difficult passages that he goes to greater length to note and discuss explanations previously propounded. Take for example what he says on the words ‫על מות לבן‬, the superscription of Psalm ix, which are a *crux interpretum*. At the same time the reader will observe how ancient are certain interpretations of modern exegetes. Rashi begins by refuting those who allege that David wrote this Psalm on the death of his son Absalom; for in that case ‫הבן‬ and not ‫לבן‬ would have been necessary, and nothing in the text bears out this explanation. Others transposed the letters of ‫לבן‬ to read ‫נבל‬, but there is no reference to Nabal in this Psalm. Others again, like the Great Massorah, make a single word of ‫עלמות‬. Menahem and Dunash,[52] each proposes an explanation which seems to be incorrect. The *Pesikta,* in view of verse 6, thinks the Psalm refers to Amalek and Esau; and this, too, is not satisfying. Finally, Rashi gives his own explanation,— scarcely better than the others,—that the Psalm deals with the rejuvenation and purity of Israel when it will have been redeemed from the Roman captivity.

When difficult questions are propounded by the Talmud, or arise out of a consideration of the Talmud, Rashi cites previous explanations or parallel texts. But this is exceptional. As a rule he finds with marvellous nicety and without circumlocution the exact word, the fitting expression, the necessary turn. One or two words suffice for him to sum up an observation, to anticipate a question, to forestall an unexpressed objection, to refute a false interpretation, or to throw light upon the true meaning of word or phrase. This is expressed in the saying, " In Rashi's time a drop of ink was worth a piece of gold." It was not without justification—though, perhaps, the practice was carried to excess—that for centuries commentaries were written upon these suggestive words of his under the title *Dikduke Rashi,* the "Niceties of Rashi." Even at the present day his commentaries are minutely studied for the purpose of finding a meaning for each word. In fact, because of this concise, lapidary style, his commentaries called into existence other commentaries, which set out to interpret his ideas,—and frequently found ideas that did not belong there. Though the authors of these super-commentaries were Rashi's admirers, they were scarcely his imitators.

In this regard it is of interest to compare the commentary of Rashi upon the beginning of the treatise *Baba Batra* with that of Samuel ben Meïr upon the end of the treatise, which Rashi did not succeed in reaching. An even more striking comparison may be made with the commentary of Nissim Gerundi upon the abridgment of the Talmud by Alfasi, which is printed opposite to that of Rashi.[53] Rashi's style is unmistakable, and prolixness in a commentary attributed to him is proof against the alleged paternity.

By virtue of these qualities, possessed by Rashi in so high a degree, he is true to the traditions of French literature, which is distinguished for simplicity and clearness among all literatures. Besides, he compares with the French writers of the middle ages in his disregard of "style." It is true, he handles with ease Hebrew and Aramaic, or, rather, the rabbinical idiom, which is a mixture of the two. But he is not a writer in the true sense of the word. His language is simple and somewhat careless, and his writing lacks all traces of esthetic quality.

*   *   *   *   *   *   *   *

Since the Bible and the Talmud made appeal to
readers of another time and another language than those
in which they were written, Rashi's first duty was to
explain them, then, if necessary, translate them, now to
add clearness to the explanation, now to do away with
it wholly. These translations, sometimes bearing upon
entire passages, more often upon single words, were
called glosses, Hebrew *laazim* (better, *leazim*), the plural
of *laaz*. They were French words transcribed into
Hebrew characters, and they formed an integral part of
the text. Rashi had recourse to them in his teaching
when the precise Hebrew expression was lacking, or
when he explained difficult terms, especially technical
terms of arts and crafts. The use of a French word
saved him a long circumlocution. Sometimes, the laaz
followed a definition or description, in a striking
manner giving the meaning of the word or expression.

In employing these French laazim, Rashi introduced
no innovation. His predecessors, especially his masters,
had already made use of them, perhaps in imitation of
the Christian commentators, who likewise inserted
words of the vernacular in their Latin explanations.
The Latin-speaking clergy were often forced to employ
the common speech for instructing the people; and in
the eleventh century beginnings were made in the translation of the Old and New Testament by the
rendition of important passages. But while it per-
turbed the Church to see the Scriptures spread too
freely before the gaze of the layman, the rabbis never
feared that the ordinary Jew might know his Bible too
well, and they availed themselves of the laazim without
scruple. The frequent occurrence of the laazim is one of

a number of proofs that French was the current speech of the Jews of France. Hebrew, like Latin among the Christian clergy, was merely the language of literature and of the liturgy. It is noteworthy that the treatises containing most laazim bear upon questions affecting the common acts of daily life—upon the observance of the Sabbath (treatise *Shabbat*), upon the dietary laws, (*Ḥullin*), and upon laws concerning the relations of Jews with non-Jews (*Abodah Zarah*). Rashi extended the use of the laazim, developing this mode of explanation; and the commentaries of his disciples, who continued his method, are strewn with French words, which were then inserted in the Hebrew-French glossaries. Several of these glossaries are about to be published. After Rashi's commentaries became a classic wherever there were Jews, the laazim were often translated into a foreign language, as into German or Italian. The Pseudo-Rashi on Alfasi,⁶⁴ following the manuscripts, sometimes presents a German translation now with, now without the French word.

Rashi's Biblical and Talmudic commentaries contain 3157 laazim, of which 967 occur in the Biblical commentaries and 2190 in the Talmudic, forming in the two commentaries together a vocabulary of about two thousand different words. In the Biblical commentaries, concerned, as a rule, not so much with the explanation of the meaning of a word as with its grammatical form, the laazim reproduce the person, tense, or gender of the Hebrew word; in the Talmudic commentaries, where the difficulty resides in the very sense of the word, the laazim give a translation without regard to grammatical form.

At the present time these laazim are of interest to us,
not only as the expression of Rashi's ideas, but also as
vehicles of information concerning the old French. As
early an investigator as Zunz remarked that if one could
restore them to their original form, they would serve
as a lexicon of the French language at the time of
the Crusades. But even Zunz did not realize the full
value to be extracted from them. The rare specimens
that we possess of the *langue d'oïl* [55] of the eleventh
century belong to the Norman dialect and to the
language of poetry. Written, as they were, in Champagne, the laazim of Rashi represent almost the pure
French (the language spoken in Champagne lay
between the dialect of the Ile-de-France and that of
Lorraine [56]), and, what is more, they were words in
common use among the people, for they generally
designated objects of daily use. These laazim, then,
constitute a document of the highest importance for the
reconstruction of old French, as much from a phonetic
and morphologic point of view, as from the point of
view of lexicography; for the Hebrew transcription
fixes to a nicety the pronunciation of the word because
of the richness of the Hebrew in vowels and because of
the strict observance of the rules of transcription.
Moreover, in the matter of lexicography the laazim
offer useful material for the history of certain words,
and bring to our knowledge popular words not to be
found in literary and official texts. In the case of
many of these terms, their appearance in Rashi is the
earliest known; otherwise they occur only at a later date.
And it is not difficult to put the laazim back into French,
because of the well-defined system of transcription

employed. Even the laws of declension (or what remained of declension in the old French) are observed.

Unfortunately, the great use made of Rashi's commentaries necessitated a large number of copies, and frequent copying produced many mistakes. Naturally, it was the laazim that suffered most from the ignorance and carelessness of the copyists and printers, especially in the countries in which French was not the current language. Efforts have been made within the last two centuries to restore the laazim. Mendelssohn and his associates applied themselves to the commentary on the Pentateuch, Löwe, to the Psalms, Neumann, to the Minor Prophets, Jeitteles and Landau, to the whole of the Bible, and the Bondi brothers, Dormitzer, and, above all, Landau, to the Talmudic commentaries. But these authors, not having consulted the manuscripts and knowing the French language of the middle ages only imperfectly, arrived at insufficient results. Even the identifications of Berliner in his critical edition of the commentary on the Pentateuch are not always exact and are rarely scientific.

Arsène Darmesteter (1846-1888), one of the elect of French Judaism and a remarkable scholar in the philology of the Romance languages, realized that in the commentaries of Rashi " the science of philology possesses important material upon which to draw for the history of the language in an early stage of its development." With the aim of utilizing this material, he visited the libraries of England and Italy, and gathered much that was important; but his numerous occupations and his premature death prevented him from finishing and publishing his work. In the interests of French

philology as well as for a complete understanding of
the text of Rashi, it would be advantageous to publish
the notes that he collected. In fact, such a work will
appear, but unfortunately not in the proportions
Darmesteter would have given it. Nevertheless, it will
be found to contain information and unique information, upon the history, the phonetics, and the ortho-
graphy of medieval French; for the first literary works,
which go as far back as the eleventh century, the life
of Saint Alexius and the epic of Roland, have not come
down to us in the form in which they were written.
" What would the trouvères of Roland and the clerics
of Saint Alexius have said if they had been told that
one day the speech of their warrior songs and their
pious homilies would need the aid of the Ghetto to
reach the full light of day, and the living sound of their
words would fall upon the ears of posterity through the
accursed jargon of an outlawed race?" [57]

In this chapter I have made some general observations upon the composition and the method of the
Biblical and Talmudic Commentaries of Rashi. Concerning their common characteristics there is little to
add, except to remark that the explanations are generally simple, natural, and unforced. This is especially
true of the Talmudic commentaries. Rashi in large
part owes the foundations upon which his works are
built to his predecessors, and no higher praise could be
accorded him than to say that he knew the great mass
of traditions and the explanations made before him.

However, Rashi rather frequently gave his own personal explanation, either because he did not know
another, or because those propounded before him did

not seem adequate or satisfying. In the latter case, he usually put down the rejected explanation before setting forth his own. Yet there are cases in which intelligence and imagination fail to supply knowledge of some special circumstance; and such lack of knowledge led Rashi into many errors. On the whole, however, the commentaries contain invaluable information, and are of the very highest importance for Jewish history and literature, because of the citations in them of certain lost works, or because of hints of certain facts which otherwise would be unknown. Modern historians justly recognize in Rashi one of the most authoritative representatives of rabbinical tradition, and it is rare for them to consult him without profit to themselves.

CHAPTER VI

THE BIBLICAL COMMENTARIES

"Thanks to Rashi the Torah has been renewed. The word of the Lord in his mouth was truth. His way was perfect and always the same. By his commentary he exalted the Torah and fortified it. All wise men and all scholars recognize him as master, and acknowledge that there is no commentary comparable with his." This enthusiastic verdict of Eliezer ben Nathan [58] has been ratified by the following generations, which, by a clever play upon words, accorded him the title of *Parshandata,* Interpreter of the Law.[59] And, verily, during his life Rashi had been an interpreter of the Law, when he explained the Scriptures to his disciples and to his other co-religionists; and he prolonged this beneficent activity in his commentaries, in which one seems to feel his passionate love of the law of God and his lively desire to render the understanding of it easy to his people. Yet it is true that all scholars did not share in the general admiration of Rashi, and discordant notes may be heard in the symphony of enthusiasm.

Of what avail these eulogies and what signify these reservations?

If one reflects that the Bible is at the same time the most important and the most obscure of the books that antiquity has bequeathed to us, it seems natural that it should soon have been translated and commented upon. The official Aramaic translation, or Targum, of the Pentateuch is attributed to Onkelos and that of the Prophets[60] to Jonathan ben Uzziel. Rashi constantly draws inspiration from both these works, and possibly also from the Targumim to the Hagiographa, which are much more recent than the other two Targumim. Sometimes he simply refers to them, sometimes he reproduces them, less frequently he remarks that they do not agree with the text.

For the establishment of the text Rashi scrupulously follows the Massorah, the " Scriptural Statistics," the work of scholars who lived in the period between the seventh and the tenth century, and who assured the integrity of the Bible by counting the number of verses in each book and the number of times each word, phrase, or expression recurs. The Massorah soon came to have great authority; and many scholars, such as R. Gershom, for example, copied it with their own hands in order to have a correct and carefully made text of the Bible. The Massorah was Rashi's constant guide. From a calculation made of the number of times he transgressed its rules, the infractions do not appear to be numerous, and sometimes they seem to have been involuntary. As a consequence, variants from the text of the Bible are extremely rare in Rashi, and the copyists eliminated them entirely. In general at his time the text was definitely established to the minutest details, and variants, if there were any, were due to blunders of the copyists. Rashi, who probably carefully compared manuscripts, once remarked upon such faulty readings.

It is to the Massoretes that some attribute the ac-
cents which serve to mark at once the punctuation
and the accentuation of the Biblical text. Rashi naturally conformed to this system of accentuation, and if
he departed from it, it seems he frequently did so
inadvertently.

*   *   *   *   *   *   *   *

But the two great sources upon which Rashi drew
for his exegesis were the Talmudic and the Midrashic
literature, with their two methods of interpreting the
Scriptures. As a knowledge of these two methods is
indispensable to an understanding of Rashi's exegesis, I
will give some pages from the work of a recent French
exegete, L. Wogue, who presents an excellent characterization of them in his *Histoire de la Bible et de
l'exégèse biblique*:

Whatever diversities may exist in the point of view
adopted by the investigators of the Bible, in the aims they
pursued, and in the methods they employed, the methods
are necessarily to be summed up in the two terms, *peshat*
and *derash*. This is a fact which scarcely requires demon-
stration. There are only two ways of understanding or
explaining any text whatsoever, either according to the
natural acceptation of its meaning, or contrary to this
acceptation. At first glance it seems as though the former
were the only reasonable and legitimate method, and as
though the second lacked either sincerity or common sense,
and had no right to the title of method. Yet we shall see
how it came about, and how it was bound to come about,
that the Derash not only arose in the Synagogue, but assumed preponderating importance there.

From very ancient times the Pentateuch and certain chapters of the Prophets were read or translated in the synagogue every Saturday. Accordingly, the interpretation of the Law could not be slavishly literal.

Destined for the edification of the ignorant masses inclined to superstition, it perforce permitted itself some freedom in order to avoid annoying misconceptions. Sometimes the literal rendition might suggest gross errors concerning the Divine Being, sometimes it might appear to be in conflict with practices consecrated by the oral law or by an old tradition, and sometimes, finally, it might in itself be grotesque and unintelligible. Hence a double tendency in exegesis, each tendency asserting itself in the synagogue at different epochs and with varying force . . . . Two sorts of Midrash are to be distinguished; if the question concerns jurisprudence or religious practice, it is called Midrash Halakah, Halakic or legal exegesis; if the subject bears upon dogmas, promises, the consolations of religion, moral truths, or the acts of daily life, the Midrash is called Midrash Haggadah, the Haggadic or ethical exegesis. The first is intended to regulate the form and the external exercise of religion; the second, to sanctify and perfect man's inward being. Each brings to the examination of the text a preconceived notion, as it were; and it reconciles text and preconceived notion sometimes by traditional, sometimes by arbitrary, methods, often more ingenious than rational. The Peshat, on the contrary, subordinates its own ideas to the text, wishes to see in the text only what is actually there, and examines it without bias. . . . .

The pious instructors of the people felt the need of utilizing and applying to daily life as much as possible these Holy Scriptures, the one treasure that had escaped so many shipwrecks. That a word should have but one meaning, that a phrase should have but one subject, this seemed mean, shabby, inadequate, unworthy the Supreme Wisdom that inspired the Bible. The word of God was perforce more prolific. Each new interpretation of the Biblical text

added richness and new value to the precious heritage. . . .
Another very important circumstance, if it did not originate
the Midrashic method, at all events tended strongly to
bring it into vogue. I speak of the religious life, such as
it was among the Israelites, especially in the time of the
second Temple. A number of practices, more or less sacred
and more or less obligatory, were established in, or after
this period, either by rabbinical institution, or by virtue of
the oral law or of custom; and these practices, sanctioned
by long usage or by highly esteemed authorities, had no
apparent basis in the written law. To maintain them and
give them solidity in the regard of the people, it was natural
to seek to prove by exegesis *ad hoc* that the Holy Text had
imposed or recommended them in advance, if not expressly,
at least by hints and allusions . . . . The application of this
method was called forth not only by the religious practices,
but also by the ideas and opinions that had been formed or
developed in the same period. After the Babylonian Exile
the successive influence of the Chaldeans, the Persians, and
the Greeks produced among the Jews of Asia as well as
among the Jews of Egypt certain theories concerning cos-
mogony, angels, and the government of the world, which
rapidly gained credence, and were generally held to be incontestable. These theories provided a complete apparatus
of doctrines so attractive and so enthusiastically accepted
even by our teachers, that the people could not resign themselves to the belief that they were not contained in the
Bible, or, worse still, that they were contradicted by this
store-house of wisdom and truth. But these doctrines—for
the most part, at least—are not to be found in the literal
text of the Bible, and, as a consequence, the scholars turned
to the Midrashic method as the only one calculated to read
the desired meaning into the text.

Now the general character of Judaism had not
changed perceptibly during ten centuries. In the
eleventh century the Jews had the same needs as in the
first, and the same method of satisfying their needs.

They found it quite natural to bring their ideas into agreement with the Bible—or, rather, they did so unconsciously—and to twist the text from its natural meaning, so as to ascribe to the Biblical authors their own ideas and knowledge.

Yet, however great the favor attaching to this method, the Peshat was never entirely deprived of its rights. It was even destined to soar high into prominence. The appearance of the Karaites (eighth century), who rejected the Talmud and held exclusively to the Scriptures, brought into existence, either directly or indirectly, a rational, independent method of exegesis, though the influence of this sect upon the development of Biblical studies has been grossly magnified. It was the celebrated Saadia (892-942) who by his translation of, and commentary upon, the Bible opened up a new period in the history of exegesis, during which the natural method was applied to the interpretation of Biblical texts. The productions of this period deserve a commanding position in Jewish literature, as much for their intrinsic value as for their number.

While, however, in the countries of Arabic culture, natural exegesis made its way triumphantly, in the countries of Christian Europe, it freed itself from the traditional Midrash only with difficulty. Moreover, Derash— to carry a Jewish term into an alien field—was the method always employed by the Christian theologians. Throughout the medieval ages they adhered chiefly to a spiritual, allegoric, moral, and mystic interpretation. In the employment of this method the literary, grammatical, philologic, and historical aspect is perforce neglected. Nevertheless, even among Christian scholars the rational method found some worthy representatives, especially among the Belgian masters.[61]

The deplorable ease of the Midrashic method readily accounts for its vogue. The Haggadist is not compelled to hold fast to his text, his imagination has free play, and is untrammelled by the leading-strings of grammar and good sense. The task of the exegete properly so called is quite different. He may not find in the text anything which is not actually there. He must take heed of the context, of the probable, and of the rules of the language. The exegete searches for the idea in the text; the Haggadist introduces foreign ideas into the text.

"At the same time, whatever the attraction of the Midrashic method for the Jews of France and Germany, and however great the wealth of their material, neither this attraction nor this wealth could take the place of a pure, simple explanation of the genuine meaning of Scriptures, a meaning which often served as a basis for the Midrash, and in a vast number of cases would have remained obscure and incomplete. Here there was a yawning gap in an essential matter, and the man who had the honor of filling up this gap—and with marvellous success, considering the insufficiency of his scientific resources—was one of the most eminent scholars of the Synagogue, the leader of Jewish science, Rashi." [62]

It would be unjust to ignore the efforts of two of Rashi's predecessors, Moses ha-Darshan (first half of the eleventh century) and Menahem ben Helbo, who prepared the way and rendered the task easier for him. The principal work of Moses ha-Darshan, often cited by Rashi under the title of *Yesod,* "Foundation," is a Haggadic and mystic commentary, giving, however, some place to questions of grammar and of the natural construction of the text. As to Menahem ben Helbo, a certain number of his explanations and fragments of his commentaries have been preserved; but Rashi probably knew him only through the intermediation of his nephew Joseph Kara. Following the example of Moses ha-Darshan and possibly, also, of Menahem ben Helbo, Rashi used both the Peshat and the Derash in his Biblical commentaries. "Rashi," says Berliner, "employed an in-between method, in which the Peshat and the Derash were easily united, owing to the care he exercised, to choose from the one or the other only what most directly approximated the simple meaning of the text. Rashi was free in his treatment of traditional legends, now transforming, now lengthening, now abridging them or joining several narratives in one, according to expediency."

This opinion is comprehensive; but it is necessary to emphasize and differentiate.

As a rule, when the Midrash does no violence to the text, Rashi adopts its interpretation; and when there are several Midrashic interpretations, he chooses the one that accords best with the simple sense; but he is especially apt to fall back upon the Midrash when the passage does not offer any difficulties. On the contrary, if the text cannot be brought into harmony with the Midrash, Rashi frankly declares that the Midrashic interpretation is irreconcilable with the natural meaning or with the laws of grammar. He also rejects the Midrashic interpretation if it does not conform to the context. " A passage," he said, " should be explained, not detached from its setting, but according to the con-

text." In other cases he says, " The real meaning of
the verse is different," and again, " This verse admits
of a Midrashic interpretation, but I do not pretend to
give any but the natural meaning." Rashi was fond
of repeating the following Talmudic saying, which he
elevated into a principle: " A verse cannot escape its
simple meaning, its natural acceptation." Rashi, then,
cherished a real predilection for rational and literal
exegesis, but when he could not find a satisfactory explanation according to this method, or when tradition
offered one, he resigned himself to the Haggadic method,
saying: " This verse requires an explanation according
to the Midrash, and it cannot be explained in any other
way."

A few quotations will facilitate the comprehension
of this characteristic method.

1. CREATION OF THE WORLD (Genesis i. 1)

In the beginning]. R. Isaac[63] says: The Law ought to
have begun with the rule enjoining the celebration of Passover, which is the first of the Mosaic precepts. But God
" showed His people the power of His works, that He may
give them the heritage of the heathen."[64] If the heathen
nations say to Israel: You are robbers, for you have seized
the land of the seven nations (Canaanites), the Israelites
can reply: The entire earth belongs to God, who, having
created it, disposes of it in favor of whomsoever it pleases
Him. It pleased Him to give it to the seven nations, and
it pleased Him to take it away from them in order to give
it to us. *In the beginning, etc. Bereshit bara*]. This
verse should be interpreted according to the Midrash, and
it is in this way that our rabbis apply it to the Torah as
having existed " before His works of old,"[65] or to Israel,
called " the first-fruits of His increase."[66] But if one wishes
to explain these words in their natural meaning, it is

necessary to observe the following method. In the beginning of the creation of the heaven and the earth, when
the earth was confusion and chaos, God said: "Let there
be light." This verse does not set forth the order of the
creation. If it did, the word בראשנה would have been
necessary, whereas the word ראשית is always in the construct, as in Jer. xxvii. 1, Gen. x. 10, Deut. xviii. 4; [67] likewise ברא must here be taken as an infinitive ברֹא; the same
construction occurs in Hosea i. 2. Shall we assert that
the verse intends to convey that such a thing was created
before another, but that it is elliptical (just as ellipses
occur in Job iii. 10, Is. viii. 4, Amos vi. 12, Is. xlvi. 10)?
But this difficulty arises: that which existed first were the
waters, since the following verse says, that "the Spirit of
God moved upon the face of the waters," and since the
text did not previously speak of the creation of the waters,
the waters must perforce have preceded the land, etc.

Rashi's exegesis is a bit complicated, because his
beliefs prevented him from realizing that the narrative
of Genesis presupposes a primordial chaos; but his
explanations are ingenious, and do away with other
difficulties. They have been propounded again as
original explanations by modern commentators, such
as Ewald, Bunsen, Schrader, Geiger, etc. Bötticher
even proposed the reading ברא. I did not give the
preceding commentary in its entirety, because it is fairly
long and, in this respect, not typical. Consequently,
other quotations will serve a purpose.

2. THE SACRIFICE OF ISAAC (Gen. xxii. 1)

1. *After these words*]. Some of our teachers explain the
expression: "after the words of Satan," who said to God:
Of all his meals Abraham sacrifices nothing to Thee, neither
a bull nor a ram. He would sacrifice his son, replied God,
if I told him to do it. Others say: "after the words of

Ishmael," who boasted of having undergone circumcision when he was thirteen years old, and to whom Isaac answered: If God demanded of me the sacrifice of my entire being, I would do what he demanded. Abraham said: *Behold, here I am*]. Such is the humility of pious men; for this expression indicates that one is humble, ready to obey.

2. God said: *Take now*]. This is a formula of prayer; God seems to say to Abraham: I pray thee, submit thyself to this test, so that thy faith shall not be doubted. *Thy son*]. I have two sons, replied Abraham. *Thine only son*]. But each is the only son of his mother. *Whom thou lovest*]. I love them both. *Isaac*]. Why did not God name Isaac immediately? In order to trouble Abraham, and also to reward him for each word, etc.

All these explanations are drawn from Talmudic (*Sanhedrin* 89^b) and Midrashic (*Bereshit Rabba* and *Tanhuma*) sources. The meaning of the passage being clear, Rashi has recourse to Haggadic elaborations, which, it must be admitted, are wholly charming. Rashi will be seen to be more original in his commentary on the Song of the Red Sea, the text of which offers more difficulties.

3. Song of the Red Sea (Ex. xv. 1)

1. *Then sang Moses*]. " Then ": when Moses saw the miracle, he had the idea of singing a song; similar construction in Josh. x. 12, I Kings vii. 8. Moses said to himself that he would sing, and that is what he did. Moses and the children of Israel " spake, saying, I will sing unto the Lord." The future tense is to be explained in the same way as in Josh. x. 12 (Joshua, seeing the miracle, conceived the idea of singing a song, " and he said in the sight of Israel," etc.), in Num. xxi. 17 (" Then Israel sang this song, Spring up, O well; sing ye unto it "), and in I Kings xi. 7 (thus explained by the sages of Israel: " Solomon wished to build a high place, but he did not build it "). The " yod " (of the

future) applies to the conception. Such is the natural meaning of the verse. But, according to the Midrashic interpretation, our rabbis see in it an allusion to the resurrection,
and they explain it in the same fashion as the other passages, with the exception of the verse in Kings, which they
translate: " Solomon wished to build a high place, but he did
not build it." But our verse cannot be explained like those
in which the future is employed, although the action takes
place immediately, as in Job i. 5 (" Thus did Job"); Num.
ix. 23 (" The Israelites rested in their tents at the com-
mandment of the Lord") and 20 (" when the cloud was a
few days"), because here the action is continued and is expressed as well by the future as by the past. But our song
having been sung only at a certain moment, the explanation
does not apply.

כי גאה נאה]. As the Targum [68] translates. Another explanation: " He is most exalted," above all praise, and
however numerous our eulogies, I could add to them; such
is not the human king whom one praises without reason.
The horse and his rider]. The one attached to the other;
the waters carried them off and they descended together
into the sea. רמה(hath He thrown)] like השליך ; the same
as in Dan. iii. 21. The Haggadic Midrash [69] gives this explanation: one verse employs the verb ירה, the other the
verb רמה, which teaches us that the Egyptians mounted into
the air in order then to descend into the ocean. The same
as in Job xxxviii. 6, " who laid (ירה) the corner stone
thereof " from top to bottom?

2. עזי וזמרת יה ויהי לי לישועה]. Onkelos translates: my
strength and my song of praise. He therefore explains עֻזִּי
as עֻזִּי and וזמרת as וזמרתי. But I am astonished at the
vowelling of the first word, which is unique in Scriptures,
if an exception is made of the three passages in which the
two words are joined. In all other places it is provided
with the vowel " u ", for example in Jer. xvi. 19 and Psalms
lix. 10. In general, when a word of two letters contains the
vowel " o ", if it is lengthened by a third letter, and if the
second letter has no " sheva ", the first takes an " u ": עֹז

makes עָזִי רק makes רְקִי, חֹק makes חֻקִּי, עֹל makes עֻלִּי [70] כֹּל makes כֻּלּוֹ, as in Exodus xiv. 7. On the contrary, the three other passages, namely, our passage, the one in Is. (xii. 2), and that in Psalms (cxviii. 14), have עָזִי vowelled with a short " o "; moreover, these verses do not have וְזִמְרָתִי but וְזִמְרָת, and all continue with וַיְהִי לִי לִישׁוּעָה. And to give a full explanation of this verse, it is in my opinion necessary to say that עָזִּי is not equivalent to עֻזִּי nor וְזִמְרָת to וְזִמְרָתִי, but that עָזִּי is a substantive (without a possessive suffix, but provided with a paragogic " yod "), as in Psalm cxxiii. 1, Obadiah 3, Deut. xxxiii. 16. The eulogy (of the Hebrews) therefore signifies: It is the strength and the vengeance of God that have been my salvation. וְזִמְרָת is thus in the construct with the word God, exactly as in Judges v. 23, Is. ix. 18, Eccl. iii. 18. As for the word וְזִמְרָת, it has the meaning which the same root has in Lev. xxv. 4 (" thou shalt not prune ") and in Is. xxv. 5; that is to say, " to cut ". The meaning of our verse, then, is: " The strength and the vengeance of our Lord have been our salvation." One must not be astonished that the text uses וַיְהִי (imperfect changed to past) and not הָיָה (perfect): for the same construction occurs in other verses; for example, I Kings vi. 5, II Chron. x. 17 [71], Num. xiv. 16 and 36, Ex. ix. 21.

He is my God]. He appeared to them in His majesty, and they pointed Him out to one another with their finger.[72] The last of the servants saw God, on this occasion, as the Prophets themselves never saw Him. בָאֲנוֵהוּ. The Targum sees in this word the meaning of " habitation " [73] as in Is. xxxiii. 20, lxv. 10. According to another explanation the word signifies " to adorn," and the meaning would be: " I wish to celebrate the beauty and sing the praise of God in all His creatures," as it is developed in the Song of Songs; see v. 9 *et seq*.[74] *My father's God*]. He is; *and I will exalt Him. My father's God*]. I am not the first who received this consecration; but on the contrary His holiness and His divinity have continued to rest upon me from the time of my ancestors.

In the above the text calls only for the embellishments of the Haggadah. In the following passage from Rashi's commentaries the place allotted to Derash is more limited.

4. Construction of the Tabernacle (Ex. xxv. 1 *et seq.*)

2. *Speak unto the children of Israel, that they bring me an offering*]. To me; in my honor. An offering (תרומה), a levy; let them make a levy upon their goods. *Of every man that giveth it willingly with his heart* (ידבנו)], same meaning as נרבה, that is to say, a voluntary and spontaneous gift.[75] *Ye shall take my offering*]. Our sages say: Three offerings are prescribed by this passage, one of a *beka* from each person, used for a pedestal, as will be shown in detail in *Eleh Pekude*[76]; the second, the contribution of the altar, consisting of a *beka* from each person, thrown into the coffers for the purchase of congregational sacrifices; and, third, the contribution for the Tabernacle, a free-will offering. The thirteen kinds of material to be mentioned were all necessary for the construction of the Tabernacle and for the making of priestly vestments, as will be evident from a close examination.

3. *Gold, and silver, and brass*]. All these were offered voluntarily, each man giving what he wished, except silver, of which each brought the same quantity, a half-shekel a person. In the entire passage relating to the construction of the Tabernacle, we do not see that more silver was needed; this is shown by Ex. xxxviii. 27. The rest of the silver, voluntarily offered, was used for making the sacred vessels.

4. תכלת]. Wool dyed in the blood of the *halazon*[77] and of a greenish color. וארגמן]. Wool dyed with a sort of coloring matter bearing this name. ושש]. Linen. עזים]. Goats' hair; this is why Onkelos translates it by מעזי, but not "goats," which he would have rendered by עזיא.

5. *And rams' skins dyed red*]. Dyed red after having been dressed. תחשים]. A sort of animal created for the purpose and having various colors; that is why the Tar-

gum translates the word by סמגונא׳, "he rejoices in his colors and boasts of them." [78] *And shittim wood*]. But whence did the Israelites in the desert obtain it? R. Tanhuma explains: The patriarch Jacob, thanks to a Divine revelation, had foreseen that one day his descendants would construct a Tabernacle in the desert. He, therefore, carried shittim trees into Egypt, and planted them there, advising his sons to take them along with them when they left the country.

6. *Oil for the light*]. "Pure *oil olive* beaten for the light, to cause the lamp to burn always." [79] *Spices for anointing oil*]. Prepared for the purpose of anointing both the vessels of the Tabernacle and the Tabernacle itself. Spices entered into the composition of this oil, as is said in *Ki-Tissa*. [80] *And for sweet incense*] which was burned night and morning, as is described in detail in *Tezaweh*. [81] As to the word קטרת, it comes from the rising of the smoke (קטור).

7. *Onyx stones*]. Two were needed for the ephod, described in *Tezaweh*. [82] *And stones to be set*] for an ouch of gold was made in which the stones were set, entirely filling it. These stones are called "stones to be set." As to the bezel it is called משבצת. *In the ephod, and in the breastplate*]. Onyx stones for the ephod and "stones to be set" for the breastplate. The breastplate as well as the ephod are described in *Tezaweh* [83]; they are two sorts of ornaments.

If these citations did not suffice, his anti-Christian polemics would furnish ample evidence of the wise use Rashi made of the Peshat. The word polemics, perhaps, is not exact. Rashi does not make assaults upon Christianity; he contents himself with showing that a verse which the Church has adopted for its own ends, when rationally interpreted, has an entirely different meaning and application. Only to this extent can Rashi be said to have written polemics against the Christians.

However that may be, no other course is possible; for the history of Adam and Eve or the blessing of Jacob cannot be explained, unless one takes a stand for or against Christianity. It was not difficult to refute Christian doctrines; Rashi could easily dispose of the stupid or extravagant inventions of Christian exegesis. Sometimes he does not name the adversaries against whom he aimed.; sometimes he openly says he has in view the *Minim* or " Sectaries," that is, the Christians. The Church, it is well known, transformed chiefly the Psalms into predictions of Christianity. In order to ward off such an interpretation and not to expose themselves to criticism, many Jewish exegetes gave up that explanation of the Psalms by which they are held to be proclamations of the Messianic era, and would see in them allusions only to historic facts. Rashi followed this tendency; and for this reason, perhaps, his commentary on the Psalms is one of the most satisfying from a scientific point of view. For instance, he formally states: " Our masters apply this passage to the Messiah; but in order to refute the Minim, it is better to apply it to David."

One would wish that Rashi had on all occasions sought the simple and natural meaning of the Biblical text. That he clothed the Song of Songs, in part at least, in a mantle of allegory, is excusable, since he was authorized, nay, obliged, to do so by tradition. In the Proverbs this manner is less tolerable. The book is essentially secular in character; but Rashi could not take it in this way. To him it was an allegory; and he transformed this manual of practical wisdom into a prolonged conversation between the Torah and Israel.

Again, though Rashi discriminated among the Midrashim, and adopted only those that seemed reconcilable with the natural meaning, his commentaries none the less resemble Haggadic compilations. This is true, above all, of the Pentateuch. And if the Haggadah " so far as religion is concerned was based upon the oral law, and from an esthetic point of view upon the apparent improprieties of the Divine word," it nevertheless " serves as a pretext rather than a text for the flights, sometimes the caprice or digressions, of religious thought." [84] Now, Rashi was so faithful to the spirit of the Midrash that he accepted without wincing the most curious and shocking explanations, or, if he rejected them, it was not because he found fault with the explanations themselves. Sometimes, when we see him balance the simple construction against the Midrashic interpretation of the text, we are annoyed to feel how he is drawn in opposite directions by two tendencies. We realize that in consequence his works suffer from a certain incoherence, or lack of equilibrium, that they are uneven and mixed in character. To recognize that he paid tribute to the taste of the age, or yielded to the attraction the Midrash exercised upon a soul of naïve faith, is not sufficient, for in point of fact he pursued the two methods at the same time, the method of literal and the method of free interpretation, seeming to have considered them equally legitimate and fruitful of results. Often, it is true, he shakes off the authority of tradition, and we naturally query why his good sense did not always assert itself, and free him from the tentacles of the Talmud and the Midrash.

Now that we have formulated our grievance against Rashi, it is fair that we try to justify him by recalling the ideas prevailing at the time, and the needs he wished to satisfy.

The Midrashim, as I have said, have a double object, on the one hand, the exposition of legal and religious practices, on the other hand, the exposition of the beliefs and hopes of religion. So far as the Halakic Midrash is concerned, it was marvellously well adapted to the French-Jewish intellect, penetrated as it was by Talmudism. The study of the Talmud so completely filled the lives of the Jews that it was difficult to break away from the rabbinical method. Rashi did not see in the Bible a literary or philosophic masterpiece. Nor did he study it with the unprejudiced eyes of the scholar. He devoted himself to this study—especially of the Pentateuch—with only the one aim in view, that of finding the origin or the explanation of civil and ritual laws, the basis or the indication of Talmudic precepts. Sometimes he kicked against the pricks. When convinced that the rabbinical explanation did not agree with a sane exegesis, he would place himself at variance with the Talmud for the sake of a rational interpretation. What more than this can be expected? Nor need we think of him as the unwilling prisoner of rules and a victim of their tyranny. On the contrary, he adapted himself to them perfectly, and believed that the Midrash could be made to conform to its meaning without violence to the text. That he always had reason to believe so was denied by so early a successor as his grandson Samuel ben Meïr. Samuel insisted that one stand face to face with the Scriptures and interpret them without

paying heed and having recourse to any other work.
This effort at intellectual independence in which the
grandson nearly always succeeded, the grandfather was
often incapable of making. In commenting upon the
Talmud Rashi preserved his entire liberty, unrestrained
by the weight of any absolute authority; but in commenting on the Bible he felt himself bound by the
Talmud and the Midrash. Especially in regard to the
Pentateuch, the Talmudic interpretation was unavoid-
able, because the Pentateuch either explicitly or impli-
citly contains all legal prescriptions. In point of fact,
in leaving the Pentateuch and proceeding to other parts
of the Bible, he gains in force because he gains in independence. He no longer fears to confront " our sages "
with the true explanation. For example, there is little
Derash in the following commentary on Psalm xxiii :

A Psalm of David]. Our rabbis say: The formula
" Psalm of David " indicates that David at first played the
instrument, then was favored by Divine inspiration. It,
therefore, signifies, Psalm to give inspiration to David. On
the other hand, when it is said " To David, a Psalm," [85] the
formula indicates that David, having received Divine inspiration, sang a song in consequence of the revelation.
1. *The Lord is my Shepherd; I shall not want*]. In
this desert in which I wander I am full of trust, sure that
I shall lack nothing.
2. *He maketh me to lie down in green pastures*]. In
a place to dwell where grass grows. The poet, having begun by comparing his sustenance to the pasturing of animals, in the words, " The Lord is my Shepherd," continues
the image. This Psalm was recited by David in the forest
of Hereth, which was so called because it was arid as
clay (*heres*), but it was watered by God with all the delights
of the next world (Midrash on the Psalms).

3. *He will restore my soul*]. My soul, benumbed by misfortunes and by my flight, He will restore to its former estate. *He will lead me in the paths of righteousness*] along the straight highway so that I may not fall into the hands of my enemies.

4. *Yea, though I walk through the valley of the shadow of death, I will fear no evil*]. In the country of shadows; this applies to the wilderness of Ziph.[85] The word צלמות here employed always signifies "utter darkness"[87]; this is the way in which it is explained by Dunash ben Labrat.[88] *Thy rod and thy staff they comfort me*]. The sufferings I have undergone and my reliance, my trust, in Thy goodness are my two consolations, for they bring me pardon for my faults, and I am sure that

5. *Thou wilt prepare a table before me*], that is, royalty. *Thou hast anointed my head with oil*]. I have already been consecrated king at Thy command. *My cup runneth over*]. An expression signifying abundance.

From this commentary one realizes, I do not say the perfection, but the simplicity, Rashi could attain when he was not obliged to discover in Scriptures allusions to laws or to beliefs foreign to the text. As Mendelssohn said of him, "No one is comparable with him when he writes Peshat." Even though Rashi gave too much space to the legal exegesis of the Talmud, Mendelssohn's example will make us more tolerant toward him —Mendelssohn who himself could not always steer clear of this method.

Moreover, the commentary on the Bible is not exactly a scholarly work; it is above all a devotional work, written, as the Germans say, *für Schule und Haus,* for the school and the family. The masses, to whom Rashi addressed himself, were not so cultivated that he could confine himself to a purely grammatical exposition or to bare exegesis. He had to introduce fascinating legends, subtle deductions, ingenious comparisons. The Bible was studied, not so much for its own sake, as for the fact that it was the text-book of morality, the foundation of belief, the source of all hopes. Every thought, every feeling bore an intimate relation to Scriptures. The Midrash exercised an irresistible attraction upon simple, deeply devout souls. It appealed to the heart as well as to the intelligence, and in vivid, attractive form set forth religious and moral truths. Granted that success justifies everything, then the very method with which we reproach Rashi explains the fact that he has had, and continues to have, thousands of readers. The progress of scientific exegesis has made us aware of what we would now consider a serious mistake in method. We readily understand why Derash plays so important a rôle in Rashi's commentaries, and to what requirements he responded; but that does not make us any more content with his method. To turn from Rashi to a more general consideration of the Midrashic exegesis, we also understand its long continuance, though we do not deprecate it less, because it is unscientific and irrational.

In spite of all, however, the use of the Derash must be considered a virtue in Rashi. Writing before the author of the *Yalkut Shimeoni*,[39] he revealed to his contemporaries, among whom not only the masses are to be included, but, owing to the rarity of books, scholars as well, a vast number of legends and traditions, which have entered into the very being of the people, and have been adopted as their own. Rashi not only popularized numerous Midrashim, but he also preserved a number

the sources of which are no longer extant, and which
without him would be unknown.   His Biblical commentary is thus the store-house of Midrashic literature, the
aftermath of that luxuriant growth whose latest products ripened in the eighth, ninth, and even tenth
centuries.

It is hardly proper, then, to be unduly severe in our
judgment of Rashi's work.   In fact, why insist on his
faults, since he himself recognized the imperfections of
his work, and would have bettered them if he had had
the time?   The testimony of his grandson upon this
point is explicit:

"The friends of reason," said Samuel ben Meïr, "should
steep themselves in this principle of our sages, that natural
exegesis can never be superseded.   It is true that the chief
aim of the Torah was to outline for us rules of religious
conduct, which we discover behind the literal meaning
through Haggadic and Halakic interpretation.   And the
ancients, moved by their piety, occupied themselves only
with Midrashic exegesis as being the most important, and
they failed to dwell at great length upon the literal meaning.   Add to this the fact that the scholars advise us not to
philosophize too much upon the Scriptures.   And R. Solomon, my maternal grandfather, the Torch of the Captivity,
who commented on the Law, the Prophets, and the Hagiographa, devoted himself to the development of the natural
meaning of the text; and I, Samuel son of Meïr, discussed
his explanations with him and before him, and he confessed
to me that if he had had the leisure, he would have deemed
it necessary to do his work all over again by availing himself of the explanations that suggest themselves day after
day." [90]

It seems, therefore, that Rashi only gradually, as the
result of experience and discussion, attained to a full

consciousness of the requirements of a sound exegesis
and the duties of a Biblical commentator. What the
grandfather had not been able to do was accomplished
by the grandson. The commentary of Samuel ben Meïr
realized Rashi's resolutions. Though Rashi may not
have been irreproachable as a commentator, he at least
pointed out the way, and his successors, enlightened by
his example, could elaborate his method and surpass it,
but only with the means with which he provided them.
We must take into account that he was almost an origi-
nator, and we readily overlook many faults and flaws in
remembering that he was the first to prepare the
material.

*   *   *   *   *   *   *   *

Grammar and lexicography are the two bases of exegesis. Rashi was as clever a grammarian as was possible
in his time and in his country. At all events he was
not of the same opinion as the Pope, who rebuked the
Archbishop of Vienna for having taught grammar in his
schools, because, he said, it seemed to him rules of grammar were not worthy the Sacred Text, and it was
unfitting to subject the language of Holy Scriptures to
these rules. Rashi in his explanations pays regard to
the laws of language, and in both his Talmudic and
Biblical commentaries, he frequently formulates scientific laws, or, it might be said, empiric rules, regarding,
for instance, distinctions in the usage of words indicated
by the position of the accent, different meanings of the
same particle, certain vowel changes, and so on. Thus,
we have been able to construct a grammar of Rashi,
somewhat rudimentary, but very advanced for the time.

Nevertheless, in this regard, a wide gap separates the commentaries of Rashi and the works of the Spanish school of exegetes, which shone with such lustre in that epoch. Under the influence and stimulus of the Arabs, scientific studies took an upward flight among the Jews of Moslem Spain. The Midrash was abandoned to the preachers, while the scholars cultivated the Hebrew language and literature with fruitful results. In France, on the contrary, though rabbinical studies were already flourishing, the same is not true of philological studies, which were introduced into France only through the influence of the Spaniards. French scholars soon came to know the works, written in Hebrew, of Menahem ben Saruk and Dunash ben Labrat,[91] and Rashi availed himself of them frequently, and not always uncritically. Thus, like them, he distinguishes triliteral, biliteral, and even uniliteral roots; but contrary to them, he maintains that contracted and quiescent verbs are triliteral and not biliteral. Unfortunately, he could have no knowledge of the more important works of Hayyuj, "father of grammarians," and of Ibn Janah, who carried the study of Hebrew to a perfection surpassed only by the moderns;[92] for these works were written in Arabic, and the translations into Hebrew, made by the scholars of Southern France, did not appear until the twelfth and thirteenth centuries. Though the Spanish Jews did not yet cultivate the allegoric and mystic exegesis, their philosophic sense was rather refined and they did not always approach the study of the Bible without seeking something not clearly expressed in the text, without *arrière-pensée,* so to speak. Rashi's exegesis was more ingenuous and, therefore, more objective.

Moreover, even if Rashi was not in complete possession of grammatical rules, he had perfectly mastered the spirit of the Hebrew language. Like the Spaniards, he had that very fine understanding for the genius of the language which arises from persevering study, from constant occupation with its literature. We have cited the sources upon which he drew; it would be unjust not to remark that he made original investigations. For example (and the examples might be multiplied) apropos of a difficult passage in Ezekiel, he asserted that he had drawn the explanation from inner stores, and had been guided only by Divine inspiration—a formula borrowed from the Geonim. He was frequently consulted in regard to the meaning of Biblical passages, and one response has been preserved, that given to the scholars of Auxerre when they asked for an explanation of several chapters of the Prophets. This fact shows that the Jews gave themselves up with ardor to the study of the Bible, men of education making it their duty to copy the Bible with the most scrupulous care and according to the best models, to the number of which they thus made additions. Among these copies are the ones made by Gershom, by Joseph Tob Elem, and by Menahem of Joigny. The Jews were almost the only persons versed in the Bible. I have mentioned how much the Church feared the sight of the Bible in the hands of the common people, and in clerical circles an absolutely anti-scientific spirit reigned in regard to these matters. It was the triumph of symbolism, allegory, and docetism. All the less likely, then, were they to know Hebrew. An exception was the monk Sigebert de Gemblours, a teacher at Metz in the last quarter of the eleventh century, who maintained relations with Jewish scholars. He is said to have known Hebrew.

Rashi's thorough knowledge of Hebrew enabled him to depend upon his memory for quoting the appropriate verses, and in all his citations there is scarcely a mistake, natural though an error would have been in quoting from memory. Distinguishing between the Hebrew of the Bible and that of the Talmud, he sees in the Hebrew of the Mishnah a transition between the two. Often, for the purpose of explaining a word in the Bible, he has recourse to Talmudic Hebrew or to the Aramaic. He pays careful attention to the precise meaning of words and to distinctions among synonyms, and he had perception for delicate shading in syntax and vocabulary. Owing to this thorough knowledge of Hebrew he readily obtained insight into the true sense of the text. By subjecting the thought of the Holy Scriptures to a simple and entirely rational examination, he not seldom succeeds in determining it. Thus, as it were by divination, he lighted upon the meaning of numerous Biblical passages. A long list might be made of explanations misunderstood by his successors, and revived, consciously or unconsciously, by modern exegetes. An illustration in point is his explanation of the first verse of Genesis, quoted above. Long before such Biblical criticism had become current it was he who said that the " servant of God " mentioned in certain chapters of the second part of Isaiah represents the people of Israel.

Needless to say Rashi never tampers with the text. At most, as is the case with Ibn Djanah, he says that a letter is missing or is superfluous. Sometimes, too, he changes the order of the words. Neither copyists' mistakes nor grammatical anomalies existed for him. Yet he believed in all sincerity that the ancient sages could have corrected certain Biblical texts to remove from them a meaning startling or derogatory when applied to the Divinity.

Rashi wholly ignored what modern criticism calls the Introduction to the Scriptures, that is to say, the study of the Bible and the books of which it is composed from the point of view of their origin, their value, and the changes they have undergone. But rarely, here and there in his commentaries, does one find any references to the formation of the canon. To give an example showing how he justified a classification of the Hagiographa given by a Talmudic text and disagreeing with the present classification: Ruth comes first, because it belongs to the period of the Judges; Job follows, because he lived at the time of the Queen of Sheba; then come the three books of Solomon, Proverbs, Ecclesiastes, both gnomic works, and the Song of Songs, written in Solomon's old age; Lamentations, Daniel, Esther, Ezra (comprising the present Nehemiah), and Chronicles are likewise placed in chronological order. In the same passage of the Talmud the question is put as to why the redaction of the prophecies of Isaiah is attributed to King Hezekiah and his academy. Rashi explained that the prophets collected their speeches only a short time before their death, and Isaiah having died a violent death, his works could not enjoy the benefit of his own redaction.

Still less need one expect to find in Rashi modern exegesis, that criticism which applies to Scriptures an investigation entirely independent of extraneous considerations, such as is brought to bear upon purely human works. Rashi's candid soul was never grazed by the slightest doubt of the authenticity of a Biblical passage. We can admire the genial divinations of an Abraham Ibn Ezra, but we also owe respect to that sincere faith of Rashi which was incapable of suspecting the testimony of tradition and the axioms of religion.

Ibn Ezra [93] and Rashi present the most vivid contrast. Though Ibn Ezra was open-minded and clear-sighted, he was restless and troubled. He led an adventurous existence, because his character was adventurous. Rashi's spirit was calm, without morbid curiosity, leaning easily upon the support of traditional religion, frank, throughout his life as free from the shadows of doubt as the soul of a child. Ibn Ezra had run the scientific gamut of his time, but he also dipped into mysticism, astrology, arithmolatry, even magic. Rashi, on the contrary, was not acquainted with the profane sciences, and so was kept from their oddities. With his clear, sure intelligence he penetrated to the bottom of the text without bringing it into agreement with views foreign to it. But the characteristic which distinguishes him above all others from Ibn Ezra is the frankness of his nature. He never seemed desirous of knowing what he did not know, nor of believing what he did not believe. Finally, and in the regard that specially interests us, Ibn Ezra, who belonged to the school of Arabic philosophers and scholars, who knew the Spanish grammarians, and was their inheritor, always employed the Peshat—that is, when he was not biassed by his philosophic ideas. In this case he saw the true meaning of the text, perhaps more clearly than any other Jewish commentator. Rashi did not possess the same scientific resources. He knew only the Talmud and the Midrash, and believed that all science was included in them. Moreover, though he stated in so many words his preference for a literal and natural interpretation of the text, he fell short of always obeying his own principle.

*   *   *   *   *   *   *   *

There is one characteristic of Rashi's Bible commentaries which I have already touched upon, but to which it is well to revert by way of conclusion, since it makes the final impression upon a student of the commentaries. I refer to a certain intimacy or informality of the work, a certain easy way of taking things. The author used no method. Now he explains the text simply and naturally; now he enjoys adorning it with fanciful embellishments. One would say of him, as of many an author of the Talmud, that in writing his work he rested from his Talmudic studies; and one seems to hear in these unceremonious conversations, these unpretentious homilies, the same note that even in the present day is sometimes struck in synagogues on Saturday afternoons. What clearly shows that Rashi unbent a little in composing his Biblical commentaries are the flashes of wit and humor lighting them, the display of his native grace of character, his smiling geniality. If he yielded some credence to the most naïve inventions, this does not mean that he was always and entirely their dupe. They simply gave him the utmost delight. He did not refrain from piquant allusions; and the commentary on the Pentateuch presents a number of pleasantries, some of which are a bit highly-spiced for modern taste. Fundamentally, they are a heritage of the old Midrashic spirit grafted upon the gaiety of " mischievous and fine Champagne," as Michelet said. Assuredly, there were hours in which good humor reigned over master and pupils, and we seem to see the smile that accompanied the witty sallies, and the radiance of that kindly charm which illuminated the dry juridic discussions. All this forms an attractive whole, and everyone may feel the attraction; for the commentaries on the Bible, which can be read with pleasure and without mental fatigue, are intelligible to persons of most mediocre mind and cultivation. The words of a certain French critic upon another writer of Champagne, La Fontaine, might be applied to Rashi, though a comparison between a poet and a commentator may not be pressed to the utmost. " He is the milk of our early years, the bread of the adult, the last meal of the old man. He is the familiar genius of every hearth."

For many centuries the Biblical commentaries held a position—and still hold it—similar to that of La Fontaine's Fables. Few works have ever been copied, printed, and commented upon to the same extent. Immediately upon their appearance, they became popular in the strongest sense of the word. They cast into the shade the work of his disciples, which according to modern judgment are superior. Preachers introduced some commentaries of his into their sermons, and made his words the subject of their instruction; and Rashi was taught even to the children. The mass of readers assimilated the Halakic and Haggadic elements. Those who were not students, through Rashi got a smattering of a literature that would otherwise have been inaccessible to them; and the commentaries threw into circulation a large number of legends, which became the common property of the Jews. Rashi's expressions and phrases entered into current speech, especially those happy formulas which impress themselves on the memory. His commentary is printed in all the rabbinical Bibles; it has become to the Jews inseparable from the text, and even Mendelssohn's commentary, which has all of Rashi's good qualities and none of his faults, did not succeed in eclipsing it. In short, it is a classic.

CHAPTER VII

THE TALMUDIC COMMENTARIES

The commentaries on the Bible, especially those on the Pentateuch, constitute a work for general reading and for devotion as well as for scientific study. Their general scope explains both their excellencies and their defects. On the other hand, the commentary on the Talmud is an academic work. It originated in the school of Rashi, and was elaborated there during a long time. The one is a popular work for the use of the masses, the other, a learned treatise for the use of students. The explanation of the Scriptures was written for the benefit of the faithful in popular, attractive, and comprehensible form; the explanation of the Talmud constituted matter for serious study in the academies. Or, rather, after the long, exhaustive, and often dry-as-dust Talmudic discussion, the master took pleasure in interrupting his instruction in the school to give his interpretation of Biblical passages.

This is the reason why the Talmudic commentaries," which are, as it were, the summing-up of Rashi's teachings, of his own studies, and of the observations of his pupils, have a more mature, more thoughtful character than the Biblical commentaries. They undoubtedly represent a greater amount of labor. It seems that Rashi himself made two or three recensions of his commentary, at least for many of the Talmudic treatises.

Testimony to this fact is given by the variations of certain passages in the extant text and that cited by the ancient authors, notably the Tossafists. Moreover, the Tossafists explicitly mention corrections made by Rashi in his own work. The query naturally arises whether the corrections indicate that Rashi worked the entire commentary over and over again. The answer is no; for certain treatises remained incomplete, and others seem never to have been begun. Presumably, then, Rashi revised a treatise according to the needs of the occasion, as, for instance, when it came under his eyes in the course of instruction. However that may be, the work that we now possess is a mixture of the first and the last recension, though we cannot always tell which is the later and which the earlier.

Another fact explains the difference I have pointed out between the Biblical and the Talmudic commentaries. For the Biblical commentaries there had been no precedent, and if they possess the merit of originality, they also illustrate the errors of a man who tries his powers in a field of work devoid of all tradition. For the Talmudic commentaries, on the contrary, models were not lacking. The example of Gershom was sufficiently notable to evoke imitation, though his work was not so complete as to discourage it. We must not forget Rashi's predecessors because he eclipsed them. This would be contrary to his intentions, since he frequently cites them, rendering value in return for value received. In fact, he knew well how to use their works to advantage. He submitted them to a judicial and minute examination, collecting all the material he needed furnished by the Geonim as well as by his immediate masters. It would be as inexact to assert that he only made a *résumé* of their works as to say that he worked along entirely original lines and relied solely upon his own resources. If we could compare his commentaries with previous commentaries (for some this comparison has been made), we should be forced into the admission that his part is smaller than one would suppose. The best proof of this fact is that the usual basis of his commentary for each treatise was the explanation of the master under whom he had studied it. He often cites the writings of his masters, to which he gives the title *Yesod*, "Foundation," probably either collections made by the teachers themselves or notebooks edited by their pupils. As a result of the love of brevity which is one of Rashi's marked characteristics, he does not quote in its entirety the source upon which he draws, but more frequently reproduces the sense rather than the exact words.

I must hasten to add that the Talmudic commentaries of Rashi's masters were inadequate, and did not meet all needs. We can judge of the lacunae in them both from the commentaries that have been preserved and from the criticisms which Rashi frequently added as an accompaniment to his citations. Sometimes the commentaries were too diffuse, sometimes too concise; their language was obscure and awkward; no stress was laid upon explaining all details, and the commentaries themselves stood in need of explanation; they addressed themselves to accomplished Talmudists rather than to students. Rashi's commentaries, on the contrary, could be understood by men of small learning—hence their influence and popularity. Moreover, the commentaries

of his masters often contradicted one another, coming
as they did from scholars who did not shrink from discussion.   Rashi wished to put an end to these debates
and introduce some unity into rabbinical tradition,
and generally his purpose in refraining from a quotation of his predecessors was exactly to avoid an opening
into the field of controversy.   Finally, their commentaries, it seems, were not comprehensive; they bore upon
only one or several treatises; whereas Rashi's bore on all
or nearly all the treatises of the Gemara.[95]   With Rashi
execution rose to the height of his conception.

Rashi availed himself so little of the work of his
masters that he began by establishing a correct text of
the Talmud and subjecting it to a severe revision.   The
mistakes of his predecessors oftenest arose from the
faultiness of the texts, marred by ignorant copyists or
presumptuous readers.   What is more, the use to which
the Talmud was put in the academies and the discussions
to which it gave rise, far from sheltering it from alterations made by way of correction, modified it in every
conceivable fashion, according to the views of the chiefs
of the schools.   Like every book in circulation, the
Talmud was exposed to the worst changes, and this all
the more readily, because at that time no one had a
notion of what we call respect for the text, for the idea
of the author.   As rigidly as the text of the Bible was
maintained intact in the very minutest details, so lax was
the treatment of the Talmud, which was at the mercy of
individual whim.   Naturally, the less scrupulous and
less clear-sighted allowed themselves the most emenda-
tions.   Accordingly, Rabbenu Gershom felt called upon
to put a severe restriction upon such liberties.   Though

he succeeded in moderating the evil, it could not be suppressed retroactively. Rashi realized that corrections made wittingly were indispensable, and that it was necessary to clear the Talmudic forest of entangling briers. Moreover, as we learn from Rashi himself, Gershom had already undertaken the task. Rashi also tells us that he had Gershom's autograph manuscript before him, not to mention other copies he was consulting and collating. Further testimony, apart from this internal evidence, is provided by Rashi's references to texts parallel to the Talmud, among them the *Tosefta*. Sometimes he records two readings without giving either the preference, though as a rule the reasoning or the context shows that he leans one way or the other, so that his alterations, which are usually correct, do not necessarily represent the early text. When Rashi has good cause for deciding a point in a certain way, he does not pay attention to possible errors or contradictions on the part of the Talmudists. In other words, though his text may be the most rational, it is not always the most authentic.

Rashi exercised this criticism of the text to a wide extent, yet prudently. I have already mentioned what Isaac of Vienna said concerning the numerous erasures that covered an autograph manuscript of his.[96] Many readings that Rashi rejected might have been kept—in fact they sometimes were kept—by force of finesse and subtlety. His method affords a striking contrast to that of the Talmudist Hananel,[97] who either eliminates the phrases unacceptable to him or preserves them only by doing violence to the sense. Rashi, on the contrary, compared the different versions of difficult or suspicious

passages and prefers the one not requiring a subtle
explanation. It is only when no reading satisfies him
that he assumes an interpolation or an error, in this
event frequently resorting to the Responsa of the
Geonim. Needless to say, he also paid heed to the
revision of Gershom; but since he deemed that Gershom
had himself preserved faulty readings, he took up the
work again, despite Gershom's prohibition. He realized
that this careful and detailed critical revision of his
predecessor, however ungrateful the soil might appear,
was nevertheless fertile ground, and might serve as the
solid basis of a thorough commentary.

He acquitted himself of the task with such success
that his has become the official text, the " Vulgate," of
the Talmud. In fact, his disciples inserted into the
body of the Gemara the greater part of his corrections
or restitutions (but not all; and one does not always
comprehend the reasons for their choice), which have
now become an integral part of the text. Thus a
single, definite, and official text was established—a thing
of great value in assuring the stability of rabbinical
tradition in France and Germany.

From what I have already said, the reader can gather
how individual was Rashi's method. The foundation
for his commentaries, it is true, was provided by
tradition and by the instruction he received from his
masters. But over and above the circumstance that he
preserved only what seemed fitting to him, is the fact
that value attached rather to the setting given the
material than to the material itself. Herein resides
Rashi's merit—and the merit is great. He was occupied
not so much in extracting from the discussion of the

Talmud the essential ideas, the principles indicating rules of practice, as in rendering the discussion comprehensible both in its entirety and in its details. He wrote a grammatical commentary which provides the exact meaning, not only of the opinions set forth, but also of the phrases and expressions employed. A Jewish scholar of our day, I. H. Weiss, who has accomplished much toward acclimatizing the scientific study of the Talmud in Eastern Europe, justly remarked—and what he says is a lesson to the rabbis of his country:

How many Talmudists are there nowadays who take pains to understand exactly the meaning of such and such a passage of the Talmud, or who are capable of explaining it grammatically? They do like the predecessors of Rashi, whose method it was to give an exposition of an entire discussion merely by simplifying its terms. They wrote consecutive commentaries, not notes; and they often failed to explain difficult words. Rashi, on the contrary, always definitely determined the meaning of the various terms.

He does this with a sure touch, and the precision of his explanations is all the more remarkable as he did not know—whatever one may say to the contrary—the Talmudic lexicon of Nathan ben Jehiel, of Rome, which was not brought to a conclusion until four years after Rashi's death. It is a favorite trick of legend to establish relations between illustrious contemporaries, especially when their activities were exercised in the same field, and tradition has made Rashi the pupil of Nathan. The idea of such a relationship, however, is purely fantastic, the two rabbis probably not having ever known each other.[98]

Rashi carried the same spirit of exactness and precision into the whole of this work—qualities indispensable but difficult of attainment; for as A. Darmesteter well says:

Whoever has opened a page of the Talmud understands how necessary is a commentary upon a text written in Aramaic and treating of often unfamiliar questions in concise, exasperatingly obscure dialectics. The language, too, is obscure, and the lack of punctuation renders reading difficult to novices. No mark separates question from answer, digressions from parenthetical observations. The phrases form only a long string of words placed one after the other, in which one distinguishes neither the beginning nor the end of the sentences.

The difficulty presented by the obscurity of the style is increased by allusions to facts and customs which are no longer known and cannot always be guessed at. Now, thanks to Rashi's commentary, a reader possessing a knowledge of the elements of the language and some slight knowledge of Jewish law, can decipher it without overmuch difficulty.

Rarely superficial, Rashi explains the text simply yet thoroughly. He sifts his matter to the bottom. His reasoning is free from subtleties and violations of the sense. This characteristic comes out in bold relief when we compare Rashi with his disciples, the Tossafists, who carry their niceties to an excess. It would be wrong to hold Rashi responsible for the abuse later made of controversy; while, on the other hand, praise is owing to him for the happy efforts he made to unravel the texts, not only for the purpose of explaining their meaning, but also to indicate possible objections and reply to them in a few words. One must marvel at the clear-sighted intelligence, the sureness, the mastery with which Rashi conveys the gist of a discussion as well as the value of the details, easily taking up each link in the chain of question and answer, pruning away superfluities, but not recoiling before necessary supplementary developments. In addition, rather than resort to forced explanations, he did not hesitate to avow that certain passages puzzled him, or that his knowledge was insufficient—a scruple not always entertained by his successors.

To determine the meaning of a text, Rashi frequently referred to parallel passages, contained not only in the Gemara itself, but also in other collections, such as the Tosefta, or the Halakic Midrashim." Sometimes the Gemara cites them, or refers to them, at other times it makes no allusion whatsoever to them. In the latter case, it may be stated, Rashi, even when he does not say so explicitly, himself found the text for comparison and was inspired by it.

Moreover, on occasion, he points out general rules to which he conforms, some of them indicated in the Talmud itself, others provided by the Geonim, and others again evolved by himself in the course of his studies. Those who are competent to judge admire the precision with which he lays down these principles. By combining them, an excellent, although very incomplete, Talmudic methodology might be drawn up.

Some examples will give a better idea than a mere description of Rashi's method. I will separate his commentary from the text of the Gemara by square brackets, so as to show how he inserts his commentary, and how perfectly he adapts it to the Gemara.

The following passages deal with the proclamation of the new moon, made by the supreme tribunal, upon the evidence of two persons who declare that they have seen the new moon.

Mishnah: If he is not known [if the tribunal does not know the witness, does not know if he is honest and worthy of confidence], they [the tribunal of his city] will send another person with him [to bear witness concerning the new moon before the great tribunal, which proclaims the new month]. At first, evidence concerning the new moon was accepted from any and every body; since the Boëthusians [100] turned to evil [this is explained in the Gemara], it was decided that only the testimony of persons who were known would be taken.

Gemara: What does "another" signify? Another individual? Does it mean that a single person is thought [worthy of confidence in declaring the first night of the new moon]? Is it not taught in a Baraita: "It once happened that a man came [to the tribunal, on the Sabbath, in order to give evidence concerning the new moon], accompanied by *his witnesses*, to testify concerning himself" [to declare him worthy of confidence]? Rab Papa replies: "Another" signifies "another couple of witnesses." This explanation seems to be the true one; for otherwise what would these words signify: "If he is not known?" If this individual is not known? But does it mean that a single person is believed [in bearing witness in regard to the new moon]? In connection with this, do not the Scriptures use the word law [in the verse: For this was a statute for Israel, and a law of the God of Jacob [101]]? Here, then, "the witness" signifies "the couple" of witnesses; similarly the previous "another" signifies "another couple." But is it quite certain that a single man is not enough? However, it is taught in a Baraita: "It once happened on a Sabbath that R. Nehoraï accompanied a witness to give evidence concerning him at Usha" [at the time when the Sanhedrin had its seat in that city, and the new moon was proclaimed there]. R. Nehoraï was accompanied by another witness, and if this witness is not mentioned, it is out of regard for R. Nehoraï [for R. Nehoraï is mentioned only that we may infer from his case that so prominent an authority inclined to leniency in the circumstances stated; but it is not fitting for us to appeal to the authority of his less important companion]. Rab Ashi replies: There was already another witness at Usha [who knew the one that was coming to give evidence], and R. Nehoraï went to join him. If this is so, what is it that is meant to be conveyed to us? This: we might have thought in case of doubt [possibly this second witness might not be at home], the Sabbath must not be trangressed; we are thus taught that one should do it, etc. (*Rosh ha-Shanah* 22*a* bottom).

The following passage deals with the *Lulab*, which is used at the celebration of the Feast of Tabernacles, and must be flawless.

Mishnah: A Lulab [referring to the palm branch; farther on it will be stated that the myrtle and the willow of the brook are dealt with separately] that has been stolen [is unfit; for it is said: [102] "And ye shall take you": what belongs to you], or is dry [we demand that the ritual be carried out with care, in conformity with the words of Scripture: [103] "I will exalt Him"], is unfit. Coming from an Ashera [a tree adored as an idol; the Gemara gives the reason for the prohibition] or from a city given up to idolatry [for it is considered as burnt down, as it is said: "And thou shalt gather all the spoil of it." [104] Now, the Lulab should have the length of four palms, as will be said farther on, [105] and since it is destined to be given up to the flames, it no longer has the desired length, being considered as burnt], it is unfit. If its end is cut [it is unfit; for it is not "beautiful"], or if its leaves have fallen off [from the central stem, and are united only by a band like the broom, in French called "escoube." [106] In this case, also, it is not "beautiful"], it is unfit. If its leaves are separated [attached to the stem, but at the top separated on each side, like the branches of a tree], it is good. R. Judah says: It should be bound [if its leaves are separated, they should be bound so that they are fixed to the stem as with other Lulabim]. The stony palm of the mountain-of-iron [the Gemara explains that these are palms] are good [they are Lulabim, although their leaves are very small and do not extend the length of the stem]. A Lulab having the length of three palms, so that it can be shaken [the Gemara explains: the stem should measure three palms, as much as the myrtle branch, and, in addition, another palm for shaking, for we require that the Lulab be shaken in the way told farther on (37b): "It is shaken vertically and horizontally," so as to exorcise the evil spirits and evil shades], is good.

Gemara: The Tanna is brief in showing [that the Lulab is unfit] without distinguishing between the first day of the festival [the celebration of which is made obligatory by the Torah] and the second day [for which the ceremony of the Lulab is prescribed only by the Rabbis, Scriptures saying "on the first day" [102]]. It must certainly refer to the dry Lulab [it may be unfit, even from a rabbinical point of view, for since it is a rite instituted in commemoration of the Temple, we require that it be practiced with care], for we require that it be "beautiful," and in this case the condition is not fulfilled. But so far as the stolen Lulab is concerned, I understand that it should not be used the first day, for in regard to the first day it is written: "And ye shall take you:" of what belongs to you; but why not the second day [whence does one know that one may not use it then?]? R. Johanan replies in the name of R. Simon ben Yohai: because then a regulation would be fulfilled through the commission of a trangression, for it is said [for we find a verse which forbids the fulfilment of a regulation through committing a transgression]: "And ye brought that which was stolen, and the lame, and the sick." [107] The stolen animal is likened to the lame; and just as it is irremediably unfit [it can never be offered as a sacrifice, because its imperfection is perpetual], so the one that is stolen is irremediably unfit [we deduce from this verse that it can never more become of use, even if there has been a renunciation; that is, if we have heard the owner renounce the object by saying, for example, "Decidedly, I have lost this purse;" although in regard to the ownership of the animal, we said, in the treatise *Baba Kama* (68*a*), that the holder became the possessor, if the first owner renounced it; however, he cannot offer it as a sacrifice upon the altar], whether this be before or after the renunciation. If before the renunciation, because the Torah says, " If any man of you bring an offering;[108] now, the stolen animal does not belong to him, but after the renunciation the holder becomes the possessor of it through the fact of this renunciation [why, then, does the prophet forbid its being used as an offering?]. Is it not exactly because this would be to fulfil a regulation by committing a transgression? R. Johanan says again in the name of R. Simon ben Yohaï: what does this verse signify: "For I the Lord love judgment, I hate robbery for burnt offering"?[109] [for the burnt offering that you bring me, I hate the theft of which you make yourself guilty in stealing these animals, although everything belongs and always has belonged to Me]. Let us compare this case with that of a mortal king, who, passing before the house of a publican, says to his servants: " Give the toll to the publican." They object and say: " But is it not to thee that all the tolls return?" To which the king replies: " May all travellers take an example from me and not escape the payment of toll." In the same way God says: " I hate robbery for burnt offerings; may My children take an example from Me and escape the temptation to theft."

It has likewise been shown [that the motive of the Mishnah in declaring the stolen Lulab unfit for use on the second day of the festival, is that it would be the fulfilment of a regulation through the commission of a transgression]. Rabbi Ammi says: etc., (*Sukkah* 29*b*).

From these two citations it is evident that Rashi does not shrink from complicated explanations, and that he does not comment on the easy passages. In the following quotation, the discussion is somewhat more difficult to follow.

Mishnah: A slave [non-Jewish] who has been made prisoner and ransomed [by other Jews] in order to remain a slave, remains a slave [this will be explained by the Gemara]; in order to be free, becomes free. R. Simon ben Gamaliel says: In the one case as in the other, he remains a slave.

Gemara: With which case do we concern ourselves? If it is before the renunciation of the right of possession [by the first master, who has bought him from the hands of the non-Jew], ransomed in order to become free, why should he not remain a slave? It is, then, after this renunciation. But, bought to be a slave, why should he remain a slave? [Understand: of his first master; why should he remain a slave, since there was a renunciation by which rights upon him as a slave have been renounced?]. Abaye says: The case under debate is always that in which the first owner has not yet renounced his rights upon the slave, and if the slave has been bought to remain a slave [on condition of being restored to his first master, or even upon condition of belonging to him who bought him], he remains the slave of his first master [the second, in fact, has not acquired him, for he knows that his master remains his master, until the master has given him up; he would, therefore, be stealing the slave]; if the slave is ransomed to become free, he is the slave neither of the first nor of the second; not of the second, since he ransomed the slave to set him free, nor of the first who possibly abandoned him and did not buy him back. R. Simon b. Gamaliel, on the other hand, says: In one case as in the other he remains a slave; in fact, he admits that just as it is a duty to ransom free men, so it is a duty to ransom slaves [it is not, therefore, to be supposed that the first master would have abstained from buying back his slave].

Raba says: We are always dealing with the case in which the first master has already renounced his right of possession. And if the slave has been ransomed in order to be a slave, he serves his second master [farther on the question will be asked, from whom the second master bought him]; if ransomed to be free, he serves neither his first nor his second master; not his second master, since he bought the slave to give him his liberty; and not the first, since he had already renounced the slave. R. Simon b. Gamaliel, on the other hand, says: In the one case as in the other he remains a slave [of his first master], according to the principle of Hezekiah, who said: Why is it admitted that he remains a slave in either case? So that it should not be possible for any slave whatsoever to deliver himself up to the enemy and thus render himself independent of his master.

It is objected: R. Simon b. Gamaliel [we have been taught] said to his colleagues: "Just as it is a duty to ransom free men, so it is a duty to ransom slaves." This Baraita is to be understood according to Abaye, who takes it that there had been no renunciation [who applies the Mishnah to the case in which there has been no previous renunciation; then the first paragraph of the Mishnah is motived by the abstention of the owner, who did not ransom his slave]: we thus explain to ourselves the expression "just as" [of R. Simon b. Gamaliel, for he does not suppose that the owner abstained, granted that it is a duty to ransom the slave]. But, according to Raba, who takes it that there has been renunciation [who applies the Mishnah to the case in which there was renunciation, and the first paragraph of the Mishnah is motived by the abstention of the owner, which is equivalent to a renunciation], this "just as" [of R. Simon b. Gamaliel, what does it signify?]. Answer: R. Simon b. Gamaliel bases his opinion upon the principle of Hezekiah [the reason of R. Simon b. Gamaliel is the principle of Hezekiah: "so that the slave should not go and deliver himself up to the enemy"]. Raba replies, etc., (*Gittin* 37*b*).

What one least expects to find in a Talmudist is historic veracity. Yet it is not lacking in Rashi, either because he was guided by ancient and authentic traditions, or because he was inspired by his clear-sightedness, or—but this is apt to have been the case less frequently— because he was well served by his power of divination. Rashi took good care not to confound the different generations of Tannaim and Amoraim, or the different rabbis in each. He knew the biographies of all of them, the countries of their birth, their masters and disciples, the period and the scene of their activity. Such knowledge was necessary not only in order to grasp the meaning of certain passages, but also in order to decide which opinion was final and had the force of law. Rashi also tried to understand, and in turn render comprehensible, the customs and the by-gone institutions to which the Talmud alludes. He gave information concerning the composition of the Mishnah and the Gemara, and the relations of the Mishnahs and the Baraitas. Because it contains all these data, Rashi's commentary is still a very valuable historical document, and Jewish historians of our days continue frequently to invoke its authority.

Yet in spite of this scattered information, the commentary is marked by certain deficiencies which indicate a deficiency in his mental make-up. When he explains an historical passage of the Talmud, he is incapable of criticising it. Apart from the fact that he would not believe legend to be legend, nor the Gemara capable of mistakes, he had neither the knowledge nor the scientific culture requisite for an historian. To be convinced of this, it is necessary to read only the following passage, in which the Talmud characteristically relates the final events before the downfall of the Jewish State. As before, I reproduce the Gemara along with the com-

mentary of Rashi; but in translating the Gemara
I anticipate what Rashi says.   It must be borne in mind
that Rashi explains in Hebrew—in rabbinical Hebrew—
a text written in Aramaic.

R. Johanan says: what signifies this verse (Prov. xxviii.
14): "Happy is the man that feareth always [who trem-
bles before the future and says to himself: provided that
no misfortune befall me if I do such and such a thing],
but he that hardeneth his heart shall fall into mischief"?
For Kamza and Bar Kamza Jerusalem was destroyed; for
a cock and a hen the Royal Tower [110] was destroyed; for
the side of a litter (ריספק) [the side of a lady's chariot,
called *reitwage* (?) in German, as is said in the chapter
"The mother and her young": [111] If thou yokest the mule to
the litter ריספק for me], Betar was destroyed. For Kamza
and Bar Kamza [names of two Jews] Jerusalem was destroyed. A man whose friend was Kamza [the name of
whose friend was Kamza] and whose enemy was Bar
Kamza prepared a banquet. He said to his servant: "Go,
invite Kamza." The servant went to Bar Kamza. Finding
him seated, the host said: "Since this man is (thou art) my
enemy, why comest thou hither? Go, leave me." The
other replied: "Since I have come, let me remain here,
and I will give the price of what I shall eat and drink."
"No," he answered [I will not let thee remain here]. "I
will give thee," he [the other] insisted, "the half of the
cost of the banquet." "No." "I will give thee the price
of the entire banquet." But he took him by the arm, and
made him rise and go out. [The expelled man] said to
himself: "Since the rabbis present at this scene did not
protest, it must be that it pleased them. Very well! I shall
go and eat the morsel [of calumny] upon them in the presence of the governor." He went to the governor and said
to Cæsar: "The Jews are revolting against thee." Cæsar
replied: "Who told it thee?" "Send to them," replied the
other, "a victim [to sacrifice it upon the altar; for we
deduce from the repetition of the word "man" (in Lev.

xvii.) that the non-Jews can offer voluntary sacrifices, like
the Israelites]; thou wilt see if they sacrifice it." Cæsar
sent a calf without a blemish, but in transit a blemish
appeared on the large lip [the upper lip], others say on
the lid of the eye (דוקין) ["tela," [112] as in Is. xl. 22
דוק], which constitutes a blemish for us, but not for the
Romans [they could offer it to their gods on the high
places, provided it did not lack a limb]. The rabbis were
in favor of sacrificing the animal in the interest of public
peace. Rabbi Zechariah b. Eukolos objected: " It will be
said that you offer imperfect victims upon the altar." Then
they wanted to kill [the messenger] so that he could not
return and report what had happened. R. Zechariah objected: " It will be said that he who causes a blemish on a
victim should be condemned to death " [it will be thought
that because he caused a blemish on the victim, and because
he thus trangressed the prohibition: " There shall be no
blemish therein " (Lev. xxii. 21), he was put to death]. R.
Johanan concluded: It is this complaisance of R. Zechariah
b. Eukolos [who did not wish to put the messenger to
death] which destroyed our Temple, burned our Sanctuary,
and exiled us from the land of our fathers (*Gittin* 55b).

This passage is less historic than legendary in character; it forms part of the Haggadic element of the
Talmud. In the explanation of the Haggadah Rashi has
preserved its method, so wise, yet so simple. Others
have attempted to be more profound in interpreting it
allegorically. Rashi, with his fund of common sense,
was nearer to the truth. His conception of the naïve
tales and beliefs was in itself naïve. Moreover, before
his time it was the legislative part of the Talmud that
received almost exclusive attention. The rabbis occupied themselves with questions of practice and with
making decisions, and they tried to unknot the entangle-
ments of the discussions for the sake of extracting the

norm, the definitive law. This is the case with
Hananel, Rashi's predecessor, as well as with Alfasi,[112]
Rashi's contemporary. Although, as we shall see, the
French rabbi had studied the Talmud for the sake of
practical needs, he adopted, so to speak, a more disin-
terested point of view. He did not pretend to write a
manual of Talmudic law, but an uninterrupted running
commentary for the use of all who wanted to make a
consecutive study of the Talmud.

In the treatise *Baba Batra* (73[a]), the Gemara having
exhausted the few observations it had to present upon
the Mishnah, which speaks of the sail of a vessel and
its rigging, falls back upon some popular narratives,
" Tales of the Sea."

Raba said [all the facts that will be recounted are in
illustration of the verse (Psalms civ. 24), " O Lord, how
manifold are thy works ! " Some of the facts show that
the righteous are recompensed in the world to come, or
they serve to explain the verses of Job that speak of large
birds, of the Behemot, and of the large cetaceans; in fact,
" even the simple conversations of the rabbis must be in-
structive "]: Some sailors reported to me what follows:
" The wave which engulfs [which tries to engulf] a vessel seems to have at its head [seems to be preceded by] a
ray of white fire [a white flame, which is a wicked angel].
But we beat it with rods (אלוותא) [rods, as in these words
' neither with a rod (אלה) nor with a lance ' in the treatise
Shabbat (63a)], which bear these words graven on them:
' I am He who is, Yah, Eternal Zebaot, Amen, Selah ' [such
is the reading of the text[114]] and then it is laid to rest "
[from its agitation].

Raba recounts: Some sailors related to me that which
follows: " Between one wave and another wave there are
three hundred parasangs [115] [it is necessary to give us this
detail, for later on it will be said that the one wave raised

its voice to speak to the other; now, one can make oneself
heard at a distance of three hundred parasangs], and the
height of a wave is likewise three hundred parasangs.
Once we were on a voyage, when a wave raised us [up
to the heavens, higher than its own height; or the heat of
the heavens is so great that it extends to a distance which
one could traverse in nearly five hundred years, the distance of the heavens from the earth[116]], so high that we
saw the encampment [the dwelling] of a little star [of the
smallest of stars]; it appeared so large to us, that one
would have been able to sow on its surface forty measures
of mustard seed [which is larger than other seeds], and
if it had raised us more, we would have been burned by its
fumes [by the heat of the star]. Then a wave raised its
voice [that is, called, just as it is said, "Deep calleth unto
deep" (Psalms xlii. 7); or it may mean angels placed over
the stars] and said to its companion: 'My companion,
have you left something in the world which you have not
swallowed up [for it had lifted itself so high, you might
have thought it had sprung from the bed of the sea and
had engulfed the world]? In that case I will go destroy
it' [on account of the sins of man]. It said [the one wave
replied to the other]: 'Behold the might of the Lord: I
cannot by one thread [by the breadth of a thread] go
beyond the sand'[that is to say: I cannot leave the bed of
the sea]; thus it is said [it is the Gemara that cites this
verse]: 'Fear ye not me?' saith the Lord. 'Will ye not
tremble at my presence, which have placed the sand for the
bound of the sea by a perpetual decree, that it cannot pass
it?'" (Jer. v. 22).

Raba says: Hormin appeared to me, the son of Lillit
[Hormin with an "n," such is the text which should be
adopted, and which I get from my father; but I have
learned from my masters that it should be read "Hormiz,"
with a "z," a word which means demon, as we see in *Sanhedrin* (39a) "the lower half of thy body belongs to Hormiz[117]], running along the edge of the wall of Mahuza
[This account makes us realize the goodness of God who

loves his creatures and does not permit evil spirits to in-
jure them; it also teaches us that one must not risk oneself
alone on a voyage]; at the same moment a horseman gal-
loped by [without thinking of evil], and he could not catch
up to him [for the demon ran so quickly, that the horseman
could not think of overtaking him].

In conclusion I will give one more extract, from the
last chapter of *Sanhedrin* (92ᵇ), which contains a vast
number of curious legends.

Our rabbis taught: Six miracles occurred on that
day [the day on which Nebuchadnezzar threw the friends
of Daniel into the furnace]. These are: the furnace
raised itself [for it was sunk in the ground, like a
lime-kiln; on that day it raised itself to the surface
of the ground, so that all could see the miracle]; the furnace was rent in two [a part of its walls was riven so that
all could look in]; הומק סורו [its height was lowered, as
in the phrase סורו רע (*Kiddushin* 82a*); another reading
הומק דוסו, like יסודו, its base was thrown. This is the
explanation taught me by R. Jacob ben Yakar; but my master [118] reads הומק סידו; the lime of the furnace melted as a
result of the great heat. Such are the explanations of my
masters. It was from the heat thrown out by the lime that
those men were consumed who cast Hananiah, Mishael, and
Azariah into the burning fiery furnace and that the golden
image of the king was transformed before his eyes]; the
image of the king was transformed before his eyes; the
four empires were consumed by the flames [the kings and
their subjects, who aided Nebuchadnezzar in casting Hananiah, Mishael, and Azariah into the fire]; finally, Ezekiel
brought the dead to life in the plain of Dura.[119]

What has been said up to this point indicates the
position taken by Rashi with regard to the Halakah.
Unlike Maimonides in his commentary of the Mishnah,
he did not as a rule concern himself with the fixation of

legal principles and practice, or with the definite solution
of questions under controversy. He confined himself to
his task of commentator and interpreter. The brevity
he imposed upon himself made it an obligation not to
enter into long and detailed discussions; for he would
have had to dispose of varying opinions and justify his
choice. He carried his principle to such an extent that
it could be said of him, " Rashi is a commentator, he
does not make decisions." [120]

But there are numerous exceptions to the rule. Often
Rashi deems it necessary to state a definite solution,
either because it has been the subject of controversies on
the part of his masters, or because it was difficult to
separate it from the rest of the discussion, or because
it served as the point of departure for another discussion. Finally, the explanation of such and such a
passage of the Talmud presupposes the solution of a
question, unless the solution changes with the explanation of the passage. When the question is left in
suspense by the Talmud, Rashi usually determines it in
the strictest sense; but when it receives contradictory
solutions, he either falls back upon analogous cases or
adduces rules of Talmudic methodology. Often, however, his conclusion is nothing else than a statement
of the practice observed in his time.

In all these cases Rashi's authority carries great
weight; so much so, in fact, as to overbalance that of
Alfasi and Maimonides. Frequent appeal was made
to it by casuists of a later date, and it would have been
invoked still oftener had his Decisions been gathered
together, like those of the Spanish and German rabbis,

instead of having been scattered through a large number of compilations.

*   *   *   *   *   *   *   *

By reason of these and other qualities the Talmudic commentaries of Rashi without doubt outweigh his Biblical commentaries. I should be inclined flatly to contradict the opinion ascribed to Jacob Tam, Rashi's grandson: " So far as my grandfather's commentary on the Talmud is concerned, I might do as much, but it would not be in my power to undertake his commentary upon the Pentateuch." The Biblical commentary is not always absolutely sure and certain, and the defects are marked. The Talmudic commentary remains a model and indispensable guide. Although numerous Biblical commentaries have been composed with Rashi's as a standard and in order to replace it, no one has dared provide a substitute for his Talmudic commentary. From an historical point of view, the value of the Talmudic commentary is no less great. At the same period, in three countries, three works were composed which complemented one another and which came to form the basis of Talmudic studies. At the time when Rashi commented on the Talmud, Nathan ben Jehiel [121] composed the Talmudic lexicon, which is still used to a great extent, while Isaac Alfasi in his Halakot codified all the Talmudic regulations. Of the three works the first was the most celebrated. The exaggerated statement was made of Rashi, that " without him the Talmud would have remained a closed book." [122] And Menahem ben Zerah [123] said : ''There was no one so illuminating, and so concise as Rashi in the commentary he wrote as if by Divine inspiration. Without him, the Babylonian Talmud would have been forgotten in Israel." The echo of this enthusiastic opinion is heard in the words of the Hebrew scholar H. L. Strack, a Christian, and the modern Jewish scholar A. Darmesteter. The one says: "Rashi wrote a commentary which the Jews hold in extraordinarily high regard and which all must concede is of the greatest value." Darmesteter wrote: "Suppress the commentary of Rashi, that masterwork of precision and clearness, and even for a trained Talmudist, the Talmud becomes almost enigmatical."

Can more be said? The commentary has become, in brief, *The* Commentary, the Commentary *par excellence, Konteros (Commentarius).*

CHAPTER VIII

The Responsa

In the previous chapter we saw that Rashi, though chiefly concerned with the mere explanation of the Talmud, nevertheless intrenched sometimes upon the domain of practice. It must not be forgotten that at that epoch the life of the Jews was based upon, and directed by, rabbinical jurisprudence and discipline. The study of the Talmud was taken up for the sake of finding in it rules for the daily conduct of existence. Apart from certain questions purely theoretic in character and having no practical application, Talmudic studies, far from being confined to the school, responded to the needs of life and were of real, vital interest. But since the Talmud is not all-comprehensive, the rabbis in drawing inspiration from its rules, from precedents it had already established, and from analogous instances contained in it, were justified in rendering decisions upon new points arising out of circumstances as they occurred. Thus, measures are cited passed by Rashi upon the payment of taxes, Christian wine, the *Mezuzah*, phylacteries, etc. These measures resulted not so much from his own initiative as from the requests preferred to him by his disciples, or by other rabbis, or even by private individuals.

The Responsa addressed by rabbinical authorities to
individuals or to communities who had submitted
difficult cases and questions to them for solution, constitute a special genus of post-Biblical literature. Not to
mention their legislative value, how precious they are
as documents in proof of the fact that no distances were
too long, no obstacles too great to prevent the people
from obtaining the opinion of a scholar! They even
sent special messengers to him, when there were no
favoring circumstances, such as a fair at the rabbi's
place of residence, or a journey to be undertaken thither
for other reasons than the purpose of the consultation.
Thus lively relations were established among the Jews
of the most widely separated countries; and an active
correspondence went on between scholars of Babylon,
Northern Africa, Spain, France, Germany, and Italy.

The circle of Rashi's connections, however, was limited
to France and Lorraine. His chief correspondents were
his teachers and their disciples.[124] It was only after
Rashi's day, when communication between the Christian
and the Moslem worlds became more frequent, that
rabbinical authorities were appealed to from all the
corners of Europe and Africa.

Though his correspondents were not so widely
scattered, the subjects touched upon by Rashi in his
Responsa are very varied in character. He was consulted on the meaning of a Biblical or a Talmudic
passage, on the text of the liturgy, on rules of grammar,
on Biblical chronology, and, especially, on new cases
arising in the practice of religion. These Responsa,
inspired, so to speak, by actualities, by the come and go
of daily affairs, introduce the reader to the material and

intellectual life of the Jews of the time, besides furnishing interesting information concerning the master's method.

One of the questions most frequently agitated regarded wine of the Gentiles, the drinking of which was prohibited to the Jews because it was feared that the wine had been employed for idolatrous libations. Cases of this kind turned up every day, because the Jews occupied themselves with viticulture[125] and maintained constant communication with the Christians. Rashi showed himself rather liberal. Though, of course, forbidding Jews to taste the wine, he permitted them to derive other enjoyment from it, the Christians not being comparable to the pagans, since they observed the Noachian laws. Rashi's grandson, Samuel ben Meïr, explicitly states in Rashi's name that the laws set forth by the Talmud against the Gentiles do not apply to the Christians.

The brother of Samuel, Jacob Tam, tells us that Rashi forbade the payment of a tax by using a sum of money left on deposit by a Christian. This decision, Jacob Tam adds, was intended to apply to the whole kingdom and, in fact, was accepted throughout France. This testifies not only to the great authority Rashi enjoyed, but also to the uprightness, the honesty of his character. Another of his qualities becomes apparent in a second Responsum treating of the relations between Jews and Christians. They carried on trade with each other in wheat and cattle. Now, the Mishnah forbids these transactions. "When this prohibition was promulgated," wrote Rashi, "the Jews all dwelt together and could carry on commerce with one another; but at present, when we are a minority in the midst of our neighbors, we cannot conform to so disastrous a measure." Rashi, it is therefore evident, knew how to take into account the needs of the moment, and accommodate rules to conditions.

Relations, then, between the Jews and their fellow-citizens were cordial. The horizon seemed serene. But if one looked closer, one could see the gathering clouds slowly encroaching upon the calm sky, clouds which were soon to burst in a storm of bloody hate and murderous ferocity. Although the change came about imperceptibly and the Jews enjoyed the calm preceding the tempest, despite this and despite themselves, they entertained a smothered distrust of the Christians. For instance, they used ugly expressions to designate objects the Christians venerated. The Christians responded in kind. The ecclesiastical works of the time are full of insults and terms of opprobrium aimed at the Jews. If one reads the narrative of the Crusades, during which the blood of innocent massacred Jews flowed in streams, one must perforce excuse, not so much real hostility toward the Christians, as the employment of malicious expressions directed against their worship. The feeling that existed was rather the heritage of tradition, the ancient rivalry of two sister religions, than true animosity. As for tolerance, no such thing yet existed. It was difficult at that time for people to conceive of benevolence and esteem for those who professed a different belief. The effect of the First Crusade upon the inner life of the communities was to create anomalous situations within families, necessitating the intervention of rabbinical authorities. The Responsa of Rashi dealing with martyrs and converts no doubt sprang from these sad conditions. A woman, whose husband died during the persecution, married again without having previously claimed her jointure from the heirs of her dead husband; but she wanted to insist on her rights after having contracted the new union. Rashi, in a Responsum, the conclusions of which were attacked after his death by several rabbis, declared that the claim of the woman was entitled to consideration.

The echo of the Crusades is heard in other instances. I have already spoken of the liberal, tolerant attitude [126] assumed by Rashi in regard to the unfortunates who deserted the faith of their fathers in appearance only, and sought refuge in that of their persecutors. He excused the hypocrisy of these weak beings, who accepted baptism only externally and in their hearts remained Jews.

In general, so far as questions in regard to lending on interest, to giving testimony, and to marriage relations were concerned, Rashi held the apostate to be the same as the Jew. He was once asked if the testimony of an apostate was valid in law. " It is necessary," he replied " to distinguish in favor of those who follow the Jewish law in secret and are not suspected of transgressing the religious precepts which the Christians oblige them to transgress outwardly. At bottom they fear God. They weep and groan over the constraint put upon them, and implore pardon of God. But if there is a suspicion that they committed transgressions without having been forced to do so, even if they have repented with all their heart, and all their soul, and all their might, they cannot bring evidence *ex post facto* concerning facts which they witnessed before they repented."

Rashi, then, was indulgent above all toward those who had been converted under the compulsion of violence, and who sincerely regretted their involuntary or imposed apostasy. On one occasion, he was asked if the wine belonging to such unfortunates should be forbidden, though they had proved their return to the Jewish faith by a long period of penitence. Rashi replied: "Let us be careful not to take measures for isolating them and thereby wounding them. Their defection was made under the menace of the sword, and they hastened to return from their wanderings." Elsewhere Rashi objects to recalling to them their momentary infidelity. A young girl was married while she and her bridegroom were in the state of forced apostasy. Rashi declared the union to be valid, for "even if a Jew becomes a convert voluntarily, the marriage he contracts is valid. All the more is this true in the case of those who are converted by force, and whose heart always stays with God, and especially, as in the present case, if they have escaped as soon as they could from the faith they embraced through compulsion."

Since internal union is the surest safeguard against persecution from without, Rashi earnestly exhorted his brethren to shun intestine strife. "Apply yourselves to the cultivation of peace," he once wrote. "See how your neighbors are troubled by the greatest evils and how the Christians delight in them. Concord will be your buckler against envy and prevent it from dominating you." In a community, doubtless that of Châlons-sur-Saône, in Burgundy,[127] there were two families that

quarrelled continually. The community had intervened
to stop the strife, but one of the two families declared
in advance that it would not submit to its decision. A
member of the other family, irritated, reproached one
of his enemies with having been baptized. Now Rabbenu Gershom, under penalty of excommunication, had
forbidden people to recall his apostasy to a converted
Jew. Rashi was asked to remove this prohibition; but
he declined, not wishing to intervene in the internal
administration of a strange community. "What am I
that I should consider myself an authority in other
places? . . . . I am a man of little importance,
and my hands are feeble, like those of an orphan. If I
were in the midst of you, I would join with you in
annulling the interdiction." From this it is evident
that the strongest weapon of the rabbinical authorities
against the intractable was, as in the Church, excommunication; but that sometimes individuals asserted,
and even swore in advance, that they would not yield to
the decree against them. Rashi considered that this
oath, being contrary to law, was null and void.

Rashi, guided by the same feelings, was pitiless in his
condemnation of those who fomented trouble, who
sowed discord in families, sometimes in their own house-
holds. A man, after having made promise to a young
girl, refused to marry her and was upheld in his in-
trigues by a disciple of Rashi. Rashi displayed great
severity toward the faithless man for his treatment of
the girl, and he was not sparing even in his denunci-
ation of the accomplice. Another man slandered his
wife, declaring that she suffered from a loathsome
disease, and through his lying charges he obtained a

divorce from her. But the truth came to light, and Rashi could not find terms sufficiently scathing to denounce a man who had recourse to such base calumnies and sullied his own hearth. " He is unworthy," Rashi wrote, " to belong to the race of Abraham, whose descendants are always full of pity for the unfortunate; and all the more for a woman to whom one is bound in marriage. We see that even those who do not believe in God respect the purity of the home,—and here is a man who has conducted himself so unworthily toward a daughter of our Heavenly Father." After indicating what course is to be pursued in case of divorce, Rashi concluded: " But it would be better if this man were to make good his mistake and take back his wife, so that God may take pity on him, and he may have the good fortune to build up his home again and live in peace and happiness."

The Responsa, providing us, as we have seen, with interesting information concerning Rashi's character, are no less important for giving us knowledge of his legal and religious opinions. As a result of the poise of his nature, and in the interest of order, he attached great importance to traditional usages and customs. Innovations are dangerous, because they may foment trouble; to abide by custom, on the contrary, is the surest guarantee of tranquillity. In casuistical questions not yet solved, he did not adopt as his principle the one prevailing with so many rabbis, of rendering the strictest decision; on the contrary, in regard to many matters, he was more liberal than his masters or his colleagues. Nevertheless, he congratulated those whose interpretation in certain cases was more severe than his own. In his scrupulous piety, he observed certain practices, although he refused to set them up as laws for others, since, one of his disciples tells us, he did not wish to arrogate to himself the glory of instituting a rule for the future. He contented himself with saying: " Blessed be he who does this." Since he stuck to the rigid observance of religion, and feared to open the door to abuses, he advised his pupils not to give too much publicity to certain of his easy interpretations of the Law.

If he did not approve of laxity, he had still less sympathy with the extreme piety bordering on folly of those whom he called " crazy saints." Enemy to every exaggeration, he blamed those who, for example, imposed upon themselves two consecutive fast days. Once when the Fast of Esther fell on a Thursday, a woman applied to Rashi for advice. She told him she was compelled to accompany her mistress on a trip, and asked him whether she might fast the next day. Rashi in his Responsum first recalled the fact that the Fast of Esther was not mentioned either in the Bible or in the Talmud, and then declared that the over-conscientious Jews who fast on Friday in order to make a feast day follow close upon a fast day, deserve to be called fools who walk in darkness.[128]

Finally, although Rashi was very scrupulous in matters of religion, he was tolerant toward faults and failings in others. Sinners and, as I have shown, even apostates found grace with him. He liked to repeat the Talmudic saying to which, in generalizing it, he gave a new meaning, " An Israelite, even a sinful one, remains an Israelite."

There is little to say concerning the style of Rashi's Responsa. In the setting forth and the discussion of the questions under consideration, his usual qualities are present—precision, clearness, soberness of judgment. But the preambles—sometimes a bit prolix—are written after the fashion prevailing among the rabbis of the time, in a complicated, pretentious style, often affecting the form of rhymed prose and always in a poetic jargon. With this exception, the Responsa do not betray the least straining after effect, the least literary refinement. The very fact that Rashi did not himself take the precaution to collect his Responsa, proves how little he cared to make a show with them, though, it is true, the custom of gathering together one's Responsa did not arise until later, originating in Spain, and passing on to Germany. As I shall immediately proceed to show, it was Rashi's disciples who collected the Responsa of their master and preserved them for us, at least in part.

CHAPTER IX

WORKS COMPOSED UNDER THE INFLUENCE OF RASHI

After having passed in review the works which are the result of Rashi's own labor and which have come down to us in the shape in which they emerged from his hands, or nearly so, several works remain to be described that present a double character; they did not spring directly from Rashi's pen, but were written by his pupils under his guidance, or, at least, as the result of his inspiration and influence. They have reached us in altered form, amplified, and sometimes improved, sometimes spoiled by various authors. The confusion reigning in these works has contributed toward an inexact appreciation of their function. From the first they were meant to be compilations, collections of rules, rather than works having a specified object.

To point out the fact once again, Rashi's pupils became his collaborators; and, it must be added, they established a veritable cult of their master. They neglected nothing concerning him; they carefully noted and piously recorded his slightest deed and gesture, on what day they had seen him, under what circumstances, how he felt that day, and how he conducted himself at the table. When a case similar to some previous one arose, they contented themselves with referring to the former and reproducing the discussion to which it had given rise.

It is to this veneration, bordering on religious devotion, that we owe the preservation of Rashi's Responsa and Decisions. Some entered into the collections of the Babylonian Geonim,—a fact which shows how highly people regarded the man who was thus ranked with the greatest rabbinical authorities,—but most of them formed the basis of several independent works: the *Sefer ha-Pardes* (Book of Paradise), the *Sefer ha-Orah* (Book of Light?), the *Sefer Issur-we-Heter* (Book of Things Prohibited and Things Permitted), and the *Mahzor Vitry*. The first work was edited at the beginning, the last, at the end, of the nineteenth century, and part of the second was introduced into the first by the editor of the first. The whole of the second has just been published by Mr. Solomon Buber. The third work, which offers many resemblances to the *Mahzor Vitry,* is still in manuscript; but Mr. Buber has recently promised us its publication in the near future, as well as a *Siddur,* or ritual, of Rashi, related to the *Mahzor Vitry* and to a *Sefer ha-Sedarim.*

In all these collections it is sometimes difficult to determine what is Rashi's handiwork, or which of his pupils is responsible for certain passages. The composition of the works is, in fact, original and merits brief characterization.

The *Sefer ha-Pardes,* though commonly attributed to Rashi himself, cannot possibly have been his work, since it contains rules, decisions, and Responsa made by several of his contemporaries, and even by some of his successors. Among others are additions by Joseph Ibn Plat or his disciples (second half of the twelfth century). But in respect of one of its constituent elements,

it was a creation of Rashi's. It was formed, in fact, by
the fusion of two collections. The author of the one
containing the customs of the three cities of Speyer,
Worms, and Mayence, must have been one of the Machirites; while the author of the other, comprising Rashi's
practices and Responsa, must have been his disciple
Shemaiah.[129]

The *Sefer ha-Pardes* is a widely-read book, and it has
been used, sometimes under other titles, by the greater
number of legal compilations made in France and
Germany. It passed through various redactions, and
the one now extant is not the most complete.

The *Sefer ha-Orah,* the redaction of which is sometimes attributed, though wrongly so, to Nathan ha-
Machiri, is a compilation of several works, which seem
to have been written in Spain at the beginning of the
fourteenth century. It consists of two principal elements; the first, German in origin, is similar to the
Pardes now extant; the second is the work of the Spaniard, Judah ben Barzillaï, of Barcelona (twelfth century). It is, of course, in the first that one finds
fragments of works which date back to the disciples of
Rashi.

The *Mahzor Vitry* is a more or less homogeneous
work. It contains rules of jurisprudence and of religious practice, Responsa by Rashi, by his predecessors,
and by his contemporaries, prayers and liturgic poems,
" Minor " Talmudic treatises, the whole divided into
chapters following the yearly cycle, and bearing upon
the various circumstances of life. The work contains
many additions due to Isaac ben Durbal, or Durbalo,
who visited the countries of Eastern Europe and was

the disciple of Rabbenu Tam (about 1150). He is wrongly considered to be the redactor of the *Maḥzor Vitry*. The author of the work is, without doubt, Simḥah ben Samuel, of Vitry, a disciple of Rashi (about 1100), who availed himself, moreover, of the works of other pupils of the master.

The *Maḥzor Vitry* is of great importance not only for the historian of Rashi, but also for the historian of Franco-Jewish culture and literature at that time. The same may be said of the *Sefer ha-Pardes*. Yet this material must be used with the utmost caution; for it has come to us in a sad condition, disfigured by the compilers and copyists, who introduced elements from various sources and different epochs. The original works disappeared during the persecutions and *autos-dafé* which followed one another in France and Germany. The redactions now extant come from Spain and Italy.

These short analyses may give an idea of the collections not yet edited; for they all stand in relation one with the other, and are in great part formed of the same elements and derived from the same material.

CHAPTER X

Poetry Attributed to Rashi

Almost immediately upon the birth of liturgical poetry in the time of the Geonim, an illustrious representative arose in the person of Eleazar ha-Kalir,[130] who came to exercise a profound influence upon his successors, and in Rashi's day this poetry attained a high degree of development. That was the time when Jews, instead of merely listening to the officiating minister, commenced to accompany him with their voices in antiphonal chants.

Like most of the rabbis of his time, Rashi wrote liturgical poems, the number of which Zunz, with more or less surety, places at seven. Three are still preserved in some rituals. According to Luria, Rashi composed more than this number.

It is fair to question whether a Talmudist is fashioned to be a poet, and whether it is possible for love of discussion and dialectics to accord with poetic sensibility and imagination. Indeed, the liturgical poetry of the Jews of France and Germany has not the least artistic value. It shows neither concern for originality, nor knowledge of composition, and the poets were strangers to the conception of art and beauty. Moreover, they imposed upon themselves rather complicated rules, the most simple forms adopted being rhyme and acrostic.

Sometimes they accomplished veritable feats of mental gymnastics, whose merit resided in the mere fact that a difficulty was overcome. Too often a play upon words or alliteration takes the place of inspiration, and ideas give way to factitious combinations.

These defects disappear in a translation, which is all the more acceptable for the very reason that it does not reproduce the vivid coloring of the original. The following, recited on the Fast of Gedaliah (אז טרם נמתחו), may serve as an example. Rashi uses certain Midra-shim in it which describe the throne of God and the heavenly court. Such poetry as there is—and there is some—is overlaid and submerged by the slow development of the thought and the painfully detailed enumerations, strongly reminiscent of the Bible. It should be said that the language of Rashi is far simpler than that of his contemporaries.

Before yet the clouds were gathered in a canopy,
Before yet the earth was rounded as a sphere,
Thou didst prepare seven in Thy abode:
The sacred Law, the splendid throne, the backslider's
    return,
Paradise in all its beauty, and insatiable hell,
The atonement place for sacrificial offerings,
And the resplendent name of him who delays to come be-
    cause of all our sins.
Two thousand years before our globe were these,
Set as jewels in the sky, whence earthward gleamed their
    light;
In the realms above they ready stand round Him en-
    throned between the Cherubim.

Firm established is the heavenly throne for the King
    supreme
Whose glory is shed upon all within His presence:
By His right hand the Law engraved with flaming let-
    ters
He caresses like a child beloved.
Toward the south lies the ever-fragrant Garden,
Hell with its ever-burning flames to the north,
Eastward Jerusalem built on strong foundations,
In the midst of it the sanctuary of God,
And in the sanctuary the altar of expiation,
Weighted with the corner-stone of the world,
Whereon is graven the Messiah's holy name
Beside the great Ineffable Name.
In the centre before Him who is the source of all bless-
    ings stands Repentance,
The healing balm for the suffering and afflicted soul,
Appointed to remove each blemish, array the repentant
    in unsoiled garments,
And pour precious oil on the head of sorrowing sinners.
Thus we all, both old and young, appear before Thee.
Wash off our every taint, our souls refine from every sin.
Backsliding children, we come to Thee as suppliants,
Seeking Thee day by day with humble, urgent prayers.
Account them unto us as blood and fat of offerings,
Like sacrificial steers and rams accept our contrite words.
O that our sins might be sunk in abysmal depths,
And Thy brooding infinite mercy bring us near to Thee.

In the first part of this poem the imagination displayed cannot be said to call forth admiration either by
reason of fertility or by reason of brilliance. Any ordi-

nary student of the Talmud and the Midrash might
have produced it. Nevertheless Rashi awakens a certain
sort of interest, it may even be said that he touches the
emotions, when he pours out all his sadness before God,
or rather—for his grief is impersonal—the sadness of
the Jew, the humble sinner appealing to the mercy of
God. When his feelings rise to their most solemn pitch,
their strong pulsations visible through the unaccus-
tomed poetic garb, the cloak of learned allusions drops
of itself, and emotion is revealed under the strata of
labored expressions. All the poems by Rashi belong under the literary form called *Seliḥot,* penitential psalms,
recited on fast days.

What has been said of the first specimen quoted applies equally to the next (יי אלהי הצבאות בורא בעליונים),
for the eve of the Day of Atonement. It would have
been more effective, had there been less emphasis and a
more consecutive development of the thought.

. . . . Of all bereft we appear before Thee,—
Thine is the justice, ours the sin,—
Our faces flushed with shame we turn to Thee,
And at Thy gates we moan like doves.
Vouchsafe unto us a life of tranquil joy,
Purge us of our stains, make us white and pure.
O that our youthful faults might vanish like passing
        clouds!
Renew our days as of old,
Remove defilement hence, set presumptuous sins at
        naught;
The purifying waters of truth sprinkle upon us,

For we confess our transgressions, we rebellious, faithless children.

*   *   *   *   *   *   *   *

O that a contrite spirit, a broken, repentant heart
Be acceptable to Thee as the fat of sacrifices!
Accomplish for the children Thy promise to the fathers.
From Thy celestial abode hearken unto us who cry to
   Thee!
Strengthen the hearts of those inclined to pay Thee
   homage,
Lend Thy ear unto their humble supplication.
Yet once more rescue Thy people from destruction.
Let Thy olden mercy speedily descend on them again,
And Thy favored ones go forth from judgment justi-
   fied,—
They that hope for Thy grace and lean upon Thy lov-
   ing-kindness.

   The final specimen (תפלה לקדמך) is still more
pathetic in its tearful contrition. The last lines even
rise to unusual beauty when they point down a shining
vista of happy, serene days.

At morn we order our prayers, and wait to offer them to
   Thee.
Not sacrificial rams we bring to Thee, but hearts contrite
   and tender.
O that the tribute of our lips might plead our cause,
When suppliants we stand before Thy threshold, watch-
   ing and waiting.
The early dawn awakens us, and our faces are suffused
   with shame.

Our hearts beat fast, we whisper softly, hoarse and
    weary with calling on Thee.
We are cast down, affrighted,—Thy judgment comes.
To Thy teaching we turned deaf ears,
And unto evil were seduced.
Rebellious were we, when Thou camest to guide us
    aright,
And now we stand abashed with lowered eyes.

         .   .

Our ruin Thou didst long past see—
Is Thy fiery wrath still unappeased?
We sinned in days agone, we suffer now, our wounds are
    open,
Thy oath is quite accomplished, the curse fulfilled.
Though long we tarried, we seek Thee now, timid, anx-
    ious,—we, poor in deeds.
Before we perish, once more unto Thy children join
    Thyself.
A heavenly sign foretells Thy blessing shall descend on
    us.
Brute force is shattered, and with night all round about,
    Thy affianced spouse, loving, yearning,
Calls on Thy faithfulness; she pleads with her eyes, and
    asks, is still she Thine,
Is hers Thy love for aye?

The uniformity and monotony of this poetry, it must
be admitted, weary the reader. The author never goes
beyond a narrow circle of ideas, and general ideas at
that. It is impossible to make out whether the allusions are to contemporaneous events, the persecutions
connected with the First Crusade, for instance, or

whether they refer to the ancient, traditional wrongs and sufferings. Nowhere is Rashi's poetry relieved by a touch of personal bias. It cannot be denied, however, that the poems testify to a fund of sincerity and enthusiasm, and that is noteworthy in a period of literary decadence, when it often happens that sincerity of sentiment fails by a good deal to find sincere expression for itself. Esthetic inadequacy should by no means be taken as synonymous with insincerity. Rashi proves, that without being an artist one can be swayed by emotion and sway the emotions of others, particularly when the dominant feeling is sadness. "The prevailing characteristic of Rashi's prayers," says Zunz, the first historian of synagogue poetry as well as the first biographer of Rashi, "is profound sadness; all of them are filled with bitter plaints." Finally, if the *Selihot* by Rashi fall far short of our idea and our ideal of poetry, they at least possess the interest attaching to all that relates to their illustrious author.

BOOK III

THE INFLUENCE OF RASHI

BOOK III

THE INFLUENCE OF RASHI

CHAPTER XI

FROM RASHI'S DEATH TO THE EXPULSION OF THE JEWS FROM FRANCE

The preceding chapters show how voluminous and varied was Rashi's work. And yet we are far from possessing everything he wrote; a number of texts have disappeared, perhaps are lost forever. But this fertility is not Rashi's sole literary merit. If the excellence of a work is to be measured not only by its intrinsic value, but also by its historical influence, by the scientific movement to which it has given the impulse, by the literature which it has called into being, in short, by its general effect, no work should receive a higher estimate than that of Rashi, for, it may be said without exaggeration, no other work was ever the occasion of so much comment and discussion, and none exerted an influence so far-reaching and enduring. From the moment of their appearance his writings spread rapidly, and were read with enthusiasm. After profoundly affecting his contemporaries, Rashi continued to guide the movement he had started. His influence upon rabbinical literature is comparable only with that of Maimonides. Indeed, it was more wholesome than his. The Talmudic codex established by Maimonides aimed at nothing less than to shut off the discussions and to give the oral law firm, solid shape. Rashi, on the contrary, safeguarded the rights of the future, and gave his successors full play. Again, not having introduced into his work philosophic speculations, he was shielded against criticism, and his renown was therefore more immaculate than that of the author of the *Mishneh Torah,* who had to undergo furious attacks.

Rashi dominates the entire rabbinical movement in France and Germany. Generally, the influence of a writer wanes from day to day; but as for Rashi's, it may be said to have increased by force of habit and as the result of events, and to have broadened its sphere. Limited at first to French, Lotharingian, and German centres of learning, it soon extended to the south of Europe, to Africa, and even to Asia, maintaining its force both in the field of Biblical exegesis and of Talmudic jurisprudence.

Since it is impossible to mention all the authors and works following and preceding Rashi, it must suffice to point out some characteristic facts and indispensable names in order to bring into relief the vitality and expansive force of his achievement, and to show how it has survived the ravages of time, and, what is more, how it has overcome man's forgetfulness—*edax tempus, edacior homo.* We shall see that Rashi directed the course of the later development at the same time that he summed up in his work all that had previously been accomplished.

" The example of a man as revered as Rashi for his piety, his character, and his immense learning was bound to make a profound and lasting impression upon his contemporaries. His descendants and his numerous disciples, pursuing with equal zeal the study of the Talmud and that of Scriptures, took as their point of departure in either study the commentaries of their ancestor and master, to which they added their own remarks, now to enlarge upon and complete the first work, now to discuss it, refute it, and substitute new views. Thus arose the Tossafot, or additional glosses upon the Talmud, and thus in the following generations arose new commentaries upon the Pentateuch or upon the entire Bible, in which the rational spirit evoked by Rashi assumed a more and more marked and exclusive form." [131]

Finally, Rashi's influence was not confined either within the walls of the Jewries or within the frontiers of France, but it radiated to foreign lands and to ecclesiastical circles.

I

It may be said without exaggeration that Rashi's Talmudic commentary renewed rabbinical studies in France and in Germany. It propagated knowledge of the Talmud there and multiplied the academies. In fact, schools were founded in all localities containing Jewish communities no matter how insignificant; and it is difficult for us to obtain any idea of the number and importance of these " Faculties," scattered over the length and breadth of Northern France, which thus became a very lively centre of Jewish studies and the chief theatre of the intellectual activity of the Occidental Jews. Its schools eclipsed those of the Rhenish countries and rivalled in glory those of Spain.

What in the first instance contributed to the success of the movement begun by Rashi, is the fact that he moulded numerous disciples—in this more fortunate than Maimonides, who was unable to found a school and who sowed in unploughed land. It was only with the lapse of time that his work little by little made its way, while Rashi through his teaching exerted an absolutely direct and, as it were, living influence. Rashi's authority was such that Troyes became the chief centre of studies. Many pupils flocked to it and there composed important works, casting into sure and permanent form the intellectual wealth they had gathered while with their master. They put the finishing touches to his work and labored to complete it, even during his life, and as though under his protection.

I have already spoken of Simḥah ben Samuel de Vitry, author of the liturgical and ritual collection, *Mahzor Vitry*.[132] Among other disciples not so well known are Mattathias ben Moses, of Paris, Samuel ben Perigoros, Joseph ben Judah, and Jacob ben Simson (1123), who lived at Paris or Falaise and wrote Responsa at the dictation of his master, and, besides commentaries, a Mahzor, and an astronomic work. He was in turn the master of Jacob Tam.

Judah ben Abraham, of Paris, aided by suggestions from his master, wrote a ceremonial for the Passover. In carrying out his task, he availed himself of the notes of his older fellow-disciple Simḥah, and his collaborator was Shemaiah, who had already worked on Rashi's commentary on Ezekiel. Besides, Shemaiah made additions to Rashi's Talmudic commentaries, and composed several commentaries under his guidance. He also collected and edited Rashi's Decisions and Responsa, serving, as it were, as Rashi's literary executor. Moreover, he was a relative of Rashi's, though the degree of kinship is not known, the evidence of authors upon the subject being contradictory. Some maintain he was Rashi's grandson, or son-in-law, or the son-in-law of his sister; according to others—and this seems more exact—he was the father-in-law of a brother of Jacob Tam.

At all events, it was Rashi's relatives who contributed most to his renown. "In regard to his family Rashi enjoyed unexampled good fortune," says Zunz. "It was not only through his disciples, but also through his family that the founder of rabbinical literature in France and Germany established his reputation, spread his works, and added to the lustre of his name." A fact which no doubt helped to assure the direction of the studies made by Rashi's descendants, is that they possessed the manuscripts written and corrected by their ancestor; and these autographs were veritable treasures at a time when books were rare and copies inexact.

One of Rashi's sons-in-law, Judah ben Nathan,[133] was a scholarly and highly esteemed Talmudist. At the suggestion of his father-in-law, he completed Rashi's commentaries and continued the work after Rashi's death, using as his chief aid the oral explanations he had received from him. The son of Judah, Yomtob, was also a good Talmudist.

The other son-in-law, Meïr ben Samuel (about 1065-1135), was originally from the little town of Rameru,[134] which through him and his sons became an important intellectual centre for more than a half-century. Meïr was a distinguished scholar whom his

sons sometimes cite as an authority. He wrote Responsa in association with his master and father-in-
law.   As I have already stated, Meïr ben Samuel
married a daughter of Rashi, Jochebed, by whom he
had four sons and a daughter, Miriam, the wife of
Samuel of Vitry.   One of the sons, Solomon, has been
known to us for only about twelve years, although he
had a reputation as a Talmudic and Biblical scholar,
chiefly the latter, having received the surname of
" father of grammarians."   His reputation, however,
was eclipsed by that of his three brothers, who have
poetically been called the three vigorous branches of
the tree of which Rashi was the trunk.   These were
Samuel ben Meïr, surnamed Rashbam, Jacob ben Meïr,
surnamed Jacob Tam, or Rabbenu Tam, and finally
Isaac ben Meïr, surnamed Ribam.   The last, who
lived without doubt at Rameru and there composed
Tossafot,[135] died during the life-time of his father, leaving seven young children.   He did not equal his brothers
either in knowledge or renown.

Samuel ben Meïr (about 1085-1158) studied under
his grandfather.   As we have seen [136] he discussed exegetic questions with Rashi, and went so far as to express
opinions in his presence concerning points of casuistry.
On Rashi's death, it seems, he assumed the direction of
the school at Troyes; but he was more prominently
identified with the academy which he, following in the
steps of his master, founded at Rameru, and which
soon became prosperous.   It was at Rameru, too, that
he wrote his valuable Talmudic commentaries.[137]   Among
his pupils are said to have been Isaac ben Asher ha-Levi,
of Speyer, and Joseph Porat ben Moses, known also

as Don Bendit. Samuel ben Meïr's was a bold, independent spirit. In some instances he sacrificed a Talmudic explanation for the sake of one that seemed more natural to him. In addition he had a fair amount of scientific and philosophic knowledge, and he was very productive in the field of literature.

But Rashbam's authority, if not his knowledge, was exceeded by that of his younger brother Jacob. Jacob Tam, born about 1100, was still a very young child when Rashi died. He studied under the guidance of his father, on whose death he assumed the direction of the academy of Rameru in his father's place. Then he went to Troyes, where he was surrounded by numerous pupils, some from countries as distant as Bohemia and Russia. One of his best known disciples was Eliezer ben Samuel, of Metz (died about 1198), author of the *Sefer Yereïm* (Book of the Pious). Other pupils of his mentioned were Moses ben Abraham, of Pontoise, to whom he wrote in particularly affectionate terms, and Jacob of Orleans, a scholar held in high regard, who died at London in 1189 in the riot that broke out the day of Richard I's coronation. A year later, in 1190, the liturgical poet and Biblical commentator Yomtob de Joigny died at York. It seems that Jacob Tam, like his successors, had to suffer from the popular hate and excesses. In fact he tells how, on one occasion, on the second day of Pentecost (possibly at the time of the troubles resulting from the Second Crusade), he was robbed and wounded, and was saved from death only through the intervention of a lord. The end of his life was saddened by the *auto-da-fé* of Blois, at which numerous Jews suffered martyrdom. He perpetuated the memory of that occa-

sion by instituting a fast day. He died in 1171, universally regretted for his clear and accurate intellect, his
piety, uprightness, amiability, and modesty. His contemporaries considered him the highest rabbinical
authority, and he was consulted by persons as remote
as in the south of France and the north of Spain. He
possessed a remarkably original, broad yet subtle intellect, and his writings display keen penetration and
singular vigor of thought. He devoted himself chiefly
to Biblical exegesis; but in this domain he obtained a
reputation less through the purely exegetical parts than
through the critical work in which he defended the
grammarian Menahem against the attacks of Dunash.[18]
His liturgical compositions and the short poems with
which he sometimes prefaced his Responsa show that he
was a clever poet, an imitator of the Spaniards. Abraham Ibn Ezra while on his rovings in France was one
of his correspondents.

However, Jacob Tam, or, to call him by his title of
honor, Rabbenu Tam,—in allusion to Gen. xxv. 27, where
Jacob is described as "tam," a man of integrity—owed
his renown to his Talmudic activity, which he exerted in
an original line of work though he was not entirely free
from the influence of Rashi. If he was not the creator of
a new sort of Talmudic literature, he was at least one
of its first representatives. Either because he considered
the commentaries of his grandfather impossible to imitate, or because he could not adapt himself to their
simplicity and brevity, he took pleasure in raising ingenious objections against them and proposing original
solutions. These explanations joined to his Decisions
and Responsa were collected by him in a work called

Sefer ha-Yashar (Book of the Just), of which he himself made two redactions. The one we now possess was put together—rather inaccurately—after the death of the author according to the second recension. The *Sefer ha-Yashar* was used a great deal by later Talmudists. It may be said to have inaugurated the form of literature called *Tossafot.*

As the word signifies, the Tossafot are " additional notes," " Novellae," upon the Talmud. They display great erudition, ingenuity, and forcible logic, and they represent a prodigious effort of sharp analysis and hardbound dialectics. The authors of the Tossafot, the Tossafists, were marvellously skilful at turning a text about and viewing it in all its possible meanings, at discovering intentions and unforeseen consequences. Their favorite method was to raise one or more objections, to set forth one or more contradictions between two texts, and then to propound one or more solutions, which, if not marked by simplicity and verisimilitude, none the less bear the stamp of singularly keen insight. In their hands the study of the Talmud became a sturdy course in intellectual gymnastics. It refined the intellect and exercised the sense of logic. Yet it would be a mistake to see in the Tossafot nothing but the taste for controversy and love of discussion for the sake of discussion. The Tossafists, even more than Rashi, sought to deduce the norm, especially the practical norm, from the Talmudic discussions, and discover analogies permitting the solution of new cases. Thus, while Rashi's commentary is devoted to the explanation of words, and, more generally, of the simple meaning of the text, the Tossafot enter into a searching consideration of the debates of the Talmud. Moreover, Rashi composed short but numerous notes, while the Tossafists wrote lengthier but less consecutive commentaries. At the same time one of Rashi's explanations is a fragment of the Tossafot explanation. Thus, the commentary of the Tossafists exists in abridged form, as it were, in germ, in the commentary of Rashi. Rashi was the constant guide of the Tossafists. His commentary, "the Commentary," as they called it, was ever the basis for their "additions." They completed or discussed it; in each case they made it their point of departure, and his influence is apparent at every turn. The species of literature called Tossafot is not only thoroughly French in origin, but, it may said, without Rashi it would never have come into existence. The authors of the Tossafot are as much the commentators of Rashi as they are of the Talmud.[139] The Tossafot bear the same relation to his Talmudic commentary as the Gemara to the Mishnah. Like the Amoraim in regard to the Tannaim, the Tossafists set themselves the task of completing and correcting the work of the master; for, despite their veneration for Rashi, they did not by any means spare him in their love of truth.

The first Tossafists, both in point of age and worth, were not only the disciples, but also, as we have seen, even the descendants of Rashi. "We drink," said R. Tam, "at the source of R. Solomon." One of the most celebrated Tossafists was a great-grandson of Rashi, Isaac ben Samuel (about 1120-1195) surnamed the Elder, son of a sister of R. Tam and grandson, on his father's side, of Simhah, of Vitry. Born without doubt at Rameru, he attended the school of his two

uncles, Samuel ben Meïr and Jacob Tam. When Jacob
Tam left for Troyes, Isaac ben Samuel took his place.
Later he founded a school at Dampierre,[140] where, it is
said, he had sixty pupils, each of whom knew one of the
treatises of the Talmud by heart. Through his departure, Rameru lost its importance as a centre of study.
He collected and co-ordinated various explanations grow-
ing out of Rashi's commentaries. Thus he established
the foundations for the Tossafot, on every page of which
his name appears.

He was the teacher of the most learned Talmudists
of the end of the twelfth and the beginning of the thirteenth century. His son and collaborator Elhanan, a
highly esteemed rabbi, died before him, some say as a
martyr. Among his disciples are said to have been
Baruch ben Isaac, originally from Worms, later resident
of Ratisbon, author of the *Sefer ha-Terumah* (Book
of the Heave-Offering), one of the first and most
influential casuistic collections (about 1200) ; Isaac ben
Abraham, called the Younger to distinguish him from his
master, whom he succeeded and who died a little before
1210; and the brother of Isaac, Samson of Sens (about
1150-1230), whose commentaries, according to the testimony of Asheri, exercised the greatest influence upon
the study of the Talmud. He was one of the most illustrious representatives of the French school, and his
authority was very great. His usual abiding place was
Sens in Burgundy, but about 1211 he emigrated to
Palestine in the company of some other scholars. He
met his death at St. Jean d'Acre.

By this time Champagne had proved too contracted
a field for the activity of so many rabbis. Flourishing

schools arose in Ile-de-France and Normandy; and it is related that at Paris, in the first half of the twelfth century, lived the scholarly and pious Elijah ben Judah, who carried on a controversy about phylacteries with his kinsman Jacob Tam. But the most celebrated Tossafist of Paris without reserve was Judah Sir Leon, born in 1166 and died in 1224, a descendant of Rashi. The school of Paris having been closed after the expulsion of 1181, Judah went to study at Dampierre under the guidance of Isaac and his son Elhanan. Among his fellow-disciples, besides the rabbis already mentioned, were Samson Sir of Coucy, Solomon of Dreux, Simon of Joinville, Abraham ben Nathan, of Lunel, and others. In 1198 Philip Augustus recalled the Jews he had expelled, and the community again prospered. Judah re-established the school, which soon assumed the first place in the list of academies. Among his numerous pupils mention is made of Moses ben Jacob, of Coucy, brother-in-law of Samson and author of the famous *Sefer Mizwot Gadol* (Great Book of Precepts), abbreviated to *Semag,* which shows the mingled influence of the *Mishneh Torah* of Maimonides and of the Tossafot of the French masters; Isaac ben Moses, of Vienna, who carried into Austria the methods and teachings of his French masters, surnamed *Or Zarua* after the title of his work, a valuable ritual compilation; and Samuel ben Solomon Sir Morel,[141] of Falaise (about 1175-1253), whose most celebrated pupil was Meïr of Rothenburg, the greatest authority of his country and his time, known for his dramatic end as well as for his great intellectual activity (1225-1293).

The successor of Judah Sir Leon was Jehiel ben Joseph, or Sir Vives, of Meaux. At this time the school is said to have counted three hundred pupils. In the disputation of 1240,[142] Jehiel ben Joseph together with Moses of Coucy, Samuel of Falaise, and another less well-known rabbi, Judah ben David, of Melun, represented the Jews. A Christian source calls Jehiel " the cleverest and most celebrated of all the Jews." When he left for Palestine in 1260 the school of Paris was closed not to be opened again.

Jehiel left behind him in France two important disciples, his son-in-law, Isaac ben Joseph, of Corbeil (died in 1280), who in 1277 published the " Columns of Exile," also called *Sefer Mizwot Katan* (Little Book of Precepts), abbreviated to *Semak,* a religious and ethical collection, which enjoyed great vogue; and Perez ben Elia, of Corbeil (died about 1295), who mentions Isaac as his master also. Perez visited Brabant and Germany, where he maintained relations with Meïr of Rothenburg. Among his pupils there was Mordecai ben Hillel, an authority highly esteemed for his decisions, who died a martyr at Nuremberg in 1298. Another master of his was Samuel ben Shneor, of Evreux (about 1225), a much-quoted Tossafist, who studied under the guidance of his elder brother Moses, editor of the " Tossafot of Evreux," largely used for the present printed editions of the Tossafot. In the second half of the thirteenth century, Eliezer of Touques compiled the Tossafot of Sens, of Evreux, etc., adding his own explanations on the margin. His work forms the chief basis for our present Tossafot to the Talmud.

As always with redactions and compilations, those mentioned here are a sign of the discontinuance of studies, worn threadbare by two centuries of intense activity. Decadence, moreover, was brought about more rapidly, as we shall see, by the misfortunes that successively befell the Jews of France.

II

Rashi's influence was no less enduring and no less wholesome in the province of Biblical exegesis. An idea of the impression he made may be gained from the fact that more than fifty super-commentaries were written on his commentary on the Pentateuch, to explain or to complete it, to defend it, and occasionally to combat it. But Rashi's influence was productive of still more than this. It called into being original works superior even to his own. His disciples shook off the yoke of Talmudic and Midrashic tradition that had rested upon him. But even when they surpassed him, it was nevertheless his influence that was acting upon them and his authority to which they appealed.

Samuel ben Meïr, diffuse as were his Talmudic commentaries, was admirably brief in his commentary on the Pentateuch, which is a model of simplicity and accuracy, and is marked by insight and subtlety. It is possibly the finest product of the French exegetic school. It sets forth general rules of interpretation, as, for instance, that the Bible should be explained through itself and without the aid of the Haggadic or even Halakic Midrash. Literal exegesis, said Samuel ben Meïr, is more forceful than Halakic interpretation. He so resolutely pursued the method of Peshat, that

Nahmanides felt justified in declaring he sometimes overdid it. The same admirable qualities exist in Rashbam's commentaries on the Prophets and the Hagiographa, in which he everywhere turns to excellent account the works of his ancestor, sometimes merely referring to them, but also combating Rashi's explanations, though in this case he does not mention Rashi.

Eliezer of Beaugency and Moses of Paris (middle of the twelfth century) were doubtless among the disciples of Samuel ben Meïr. Moses of Paris, in turn, had a pupil by the name of Gabriel.

Occasionally Rashbam did not disdain the Midrash. But the same cannot be said of his friend and collaborator Joseph ben Simon Kara (born about 1060-1070, died about 1130-1140), a nephew and disciple of Menahem ben Helbo, and the friend if not the disciple of Rashi, to whom he acknowledges himself indebted. He wrote additions to Rashi's commentaries, and on Rashi's advice wrote a part of his Biblical commentaries, several of which have been published. They enjoyed great vogue, and in certain manuscripts they are set alongside of, or replace, Rashi's commentaries. They fully deserve the honor; for, in fact, Joseph Kara surpasses Rashi and rivals Rashbam in his fair-minded criticism, his scrupulous attachment to the literal meaning, and his absolutely clear idea of the needs of a wholesome exegesis, to say nothing of his theological views, which are always remarkable and sometimes bold. He frankly rejected the Midrash, and compares the person making use of it to the drowning man who clutches at a straw. Contrary to tradition he denies that Samuel was the author of the Biblical book bearing his name.

Side by side with Joseph Kara belongs his rival and younger contemporary Joseph Bekor-Shor, doubtless the same person as Joseph ben Isaac, of Orleans, who was a disciple of Rabbenu Tam, and must, therefore, have lived in the middle of the twelfth century. His commentary on the Pentateuch, which has been published in part, is frequently cited by later exegetes, and its reputation is justified by its keen insight and its vein of odd originality. Joseph Bekor-Shor had felt the influence of the Spaniards, but he had yielded to the attractions of Talmudic dialectics, which he had acquired at a good school, although, like his master, he cites, in connection with the Bible, a certain Obadiah.

Quae secuta sunt magis defleri quam narrari possunt. In the works of the second half of the twelfth century this fault becomes more and more perceptible, and signs of decadence begin to appear. Moreover, the writings at this time were very numerous, fostering, and, in turn, stimulated by, anti-Christian polemics. The greater number of the Tossafists study the Bible in conjunction with the Talmud. Citations are made of explanations or Biblical commentaries by Jacob of Orleans, Moses of Pontoise, Isaac the Elder, Isaac the Younger, Judah Sir Leon, Jehiel of Meaux, and Moses of Coucy. All these rabbis wrote Tossafot to the Bible as well as to the Talmud. This comparative study of Bible and Talmud was continued for some time, until at the beginning of the thirteenth century intellectual activity was exhausted. Original works were replaced by a large number of compilations, all related to one another, since the authors copied without scruple and pillaged without shame.

Chief among these works, which bear the general title of Tossafot to the Torah and some of which have been printed, are *Hazzekuni,* by Hezekiah ben Manoah (about 1240), *Gan* [143] (Garden), by Aaron ben Joseph, (about 1250), *Daat Zekenim* (Knowledge of the Ancients), in which many exegetes are cited (after 1252), *Paaneah Razah* (Revealer of the Mystery), by Isaac ben Judah ha-Levi (about 1300), *Minhat Yehudah* (Offering of Judah), by Judah ben Eliezer (or Eleazar), of Troyes (1313), *Hadar Zekenim* (Glory of the Ancients; beginning of the fourteenth century), and *Imre Noam* (Pleasant Words), by Jacob of Illescas (middle of the fourteenth century).

All these works were more or less inspired by Rashi, and some, such as *Hazzekuni,* might be called super-commentaries to Rashi. But these disciples were not true to the spirit of the master. They gave themselves up to the Haggadah more than he did, and also to a thing unknown to him, Gematria and mystical exegesis. Thus this French school, which for nearly a century had shone with glowing brilliance, now threw out only feeble rays, and abandoned itself more and more to the subtleties of the Midrash, to the fancifulness of the Gematria. It almost consigned to oblivion the great productions in rational exegesis, always excepting Rashi's commentaries, the popularity of which never waned, as much because of the author's renown as because of his concessions to the Midrash.

It remained for a Christian exegete to free rational exegesis from the discredit into which it had fallen. The ecclesiastical commentators even more than the authors of the Biblical Tossafot were steeped in allegorism and mysticism; but among them were some who cultivated the interpretation of the literal meaning of Scriptures, and even appealed to Jewish scholars for explanations. Unfortunately, Rashi's works, written in a language unintelligible to the Christians, could not in any degree influence a general intellectual movement.

However, exception must be made of the celebrated Franciscan monk Nicholas de Lyra (born about 1292, died in 1340), author of the *Postillae perpetuae* on the Bible which brought him the title of *doctor planus et utilis*. Nicholas de Lyra possessed knowledge rare among Christians, knowledge of the Hebrew language, and he knew Hebrew so well that he was thought to be a converted Jew. In his works, polemical in character, he comes out against the mystical tendencies in the interpretations of the rabbis, and does not spare Rashi, even attributing to him explanations nowhere existing in Rashi's writings. But these criticisms of his, as he himself says, are "extremely rare." Moreover he does not refrain from accepting for his own purposes a large number of Midrashim borrowed from Rashi. It was from Rashi's commentaries, in fact, that he learned to know rabbinical literature—only to combat it. On one occasion he said, "I usually follow Rabbi Solomon, whose teachings are considered authoritative by modern Jews." He sometimes modified the text of the Vulgate according to the explanations of the rabbi, and his commentary on the Psalms, for instance, is often only a paraphrase of Rashi's. For this reason Nicholas de Lyra was dubbed, it must be admitted somewhat irreverently, *simia Salomonis,* Rashi's Ape. Nevertheless, he exercised great influence in ecclesiastical circles, comparable to that of Rashi among the Jews. His commentary was called "the common commentary." Possibly it was in imitation of Nicholas's work that the name *glossa hebraica* (the Hebrew commentary), or simply *glossa*, was bestowed upon Rashi's work by a Christian author of the thirteenth century, who, if not the famous scholar and monk Roger Bacon, must have been some one of the same type. Another Christian exegete of the same period, William of Mara, cites Rashi's commentary under the title of Perus. The admiration felt for Nicholas de Lyra, which now seems somewhat excessive, is expressed in the well-known proverb: *Si Lyra non lyrasset, totus mondus delirasset.* A modification of the proverb, *si Lyra non lyrasset, Lutherius non saltasset,* is not an exaggeration; for the works of the Franciscan monk were soon translated into German, and they exercised a profound influence on the leader of the Reformation when he composed the translation of the Bible, epoch-making in the history of literature as well as of religion. It is known that Luther had large knowledge of the Hebrew and a strong feeling for it, a quality he owed to Nicholas de Lyra and, through him, to the Jewish exegetes, although his scornful pride would never permit him to concede that " Rashi and the Tossafists made Nicholas de Lyra and Nicholas de Lyra made Luther."

At the time when Rashi's influence was thus extended to Christian circles, the Jewish schools called into being by his work and his teachings fell into decay on account of the persecutions that shook French Judaism to its foundations and almost deprived it of existence. This shows how firmly intellectual activities are bound up with temporal fortunes—a truth manifested in the period of growth and maturity and illustrated afresh in the period of decadence.

Even after the First Crusade, the situation of the Jews of France had remained favorable. It did not perceptibly change as a result of the various local disorders marking the Second Crusade. Nevertheless, the second half of the twelfth century witnessed the uprise of accusations of ritual murder and piercings of the host. Popular hatred and mistrust were exploited by the greedy kings. Philip Augustus expelled the Jews from his domain in 1181, though he recalled them in 1198. Yet the example had been set, and the security of the Jews was done for. The lords and bishops united to persecute them, destroy their literary treasures, and paralyze their intellectual efforts. They found the right king for their purposes in St. Louis, a curious mixture of tolerance and bigotry, of charity and fanaticism. "St. Louis sought to deprive the Jews of the book which in all their trials was their supreme consolation, the refuge of their souls against outside clamor and suffering, the only safeguard of their morality, and the bond maintaining their religious oneness —the Talmud." In 1239 an apostate, Nicholas Donin, of La Rochelle, denounced the Talmud to Gregory IX. The Pope ordered the seizure of all copies, and an investigation of the book. In France the mandate was obeyed, and a disputation took place at Paris. Naturally, the Talmud was condemned, and twenty-four cartloads of Hebrew books were consigned to the flames. The *auto-da-fé* of 1242 marks the decadence of an entire literature, the ruin of brilliant schools, and the check to the movement so gloriously inaugurated by Rashi. All the living forces of French Judaism were deeply affected.

But the fall was neither complete nor sudden. It was not until 1306 that the Jews were exiled from France by Philip the Fair, and a hundred thousand persons had to leave the country in which their nation had long flourished and to whose prosperity they had materially contributed.

The expulsion of 1306 withdrew French Judaism to the provinces directly attached to the crown. In vain were the Jews recalled in 1315 " at the general cry of the people." Only a very few profited by the tolerance shown them. After that their existence was troubled by riots, and broken in upon by expulsions. The schools, of old so flourishing, fell into a state of utter decay. About 1360 France could not count six Jewish scholars, and the works of the time show to what degree of degradation rabbinical studies had sunk. With the expulsion of 1394 Charles VI dealt the finishing stroke. Thereafter French Judaism was nothing but the shadow of itself. Having received a mortal wound in 1306, its life up to the final expulsion in 1394 was one long death-agony.

Thus disappeared that French Judaism which contributed so large a portion to the economic and intellectual civilization of its fatherland during the time the sun of tolerance shone on its horizon, but which was destined to perish the moment the greed of princes and the fanaticism of priests, hoodwinking the masses, united to overwhelm it. Nevertheless the three centuries of fruitful activity were not entirely lost to the future; and the Jews of France, who had gone in numbers to foreign lands, carried with them their books and their ideals.

III

For a long time previous to the events just recorded, Rashi and the Tossafists—the two words summing up the whole intellectual movement of the Jews of France —had brought to all Judaism the reputation of the academies of Champagne and of Ile-de-France. " Hebrew literature in France," wrote E. Carmoly, " exercised upon the Jewish world the same influence that French literature exercised upon European civilization in general. Everywhere the Biblical and Talmudic works of Troyes, Rameru, Dampierre, and Paris became the common guides of the synagogues." Rashi's commentaries, in especial, spread rapidly and were widely copied, sometimes enlarged by additions, sometimes mutilated and truncated. It is for this reason that certain commentaries of his no longer exist, or exist in incomplete form.

In view of the fact that at the beginning of the thirteenth century relations between remote countries and Christendom were rare, and that the Christian and the Mohammedan worlds had scarcely begun to open up to each other and come into contact, it is readily understood why Rashi was not known in Arabic countries in his life-time, or even immediately after his death, and why he exercised no influence upon Maimonides, who died exactly a hundred years after him. In the Orient there are no signs of his influence until the end of the twelfth century. In 1192, barely eighty years after Rashi's death, an exilarch had one of his commentaries copied; and at the beginning of the thirteenth century we find the commentator Samuel ben Nissim, of Aleppo, making a citation from Rashi.

But it is naturally in the regions nearest to France that Rashi's influence made itself most felt. The profound Talmudist, Zerahiah ha-Levi, who lived at Lunel (1125-1186), rather frequently cites " R. Solomon the Frenchman," and contents himself with merely referring to Rashi's commentary without quoting in full, a fact which shows that the work was widely spread in the Provence. A number of years later, about 1245, Meïr, son of Simon of Narbonne, wrote in his apologetic work, " The Holy War " : " The commentaries are understood by all readers, for the least as well as the most important things are perfectly explained in them. Since their appearance, there is not a rabbi who has studied without using them." I have already referred to the testimony of Menahem ben Zerah; ¹⁴⁴ to his may be added that of another Provençal, Estori Parhi, who left France in 1306 to visit Spain, and wrote an interesting book of Halakah and of recollections of his travels. About 1320, David d'Estella, philosopher and poet, wrote: " It is from France that God has sent us a bright light for all Israel in the person of R. Solomon ben Isaac." Rashi was also cited in terms of praise by the brilliant commentator and philosopher Menahem ben Solomon Meïri, of Perpignan (1249-1306), and by the casuist and theologian Jacob de Bagnols (about 1357-1361), grandson of David d'Estella.

From the Provence, Rashi's renown spread on the one
side to Italy, and on the other to Spain. His Biblical
commentary was used by Benjamin ben Abraham Anaw
(about 1240), of Rome, whose brother Zedekiah was the
author of the Halakic and ritual collection *Shibbole
ha-Leket* (The Gleaned Sheaves), a work written in the
second half of the thirteenth century, which owes much
to Rashi and his successors. The celebrated scholar and
poet Immanuel ben Solomon Romi (about 1265-1330)
seems to have known Rashi, one of whose Biblical
explanations he cites for the purpose of refuting it.
The influence of the French commentator is more
apparent in the works of the Italian philosopher and
commentator Solomon Yedidiah (about 1285-1330)
and the commentator Isaiah da Trani (end of the
thirteenth century).

Rashi's influence was more fruitful of results in
Spain, where intellectual activity was by far more
developed than in Italy. His renown soon crossed the
Pyrenees, and, curiously enough, the Spanish exegetes,
disciples of the Hayyujes and the Ibn-Janahs availed
themselves of his Biblical commentary, despite its in-
feriority from a scientific point of view. They did not
fail, it is true, occasionally to dispute it. This was the
case with Abraham Ibn Ezra, who possibly came to
know Rashi's works during his sojourn in France, and
combated Rashi's grammatical explanations without
sparing him his wonted sharp-edged witticisms. To
Abraham Ibn Ezra has been attributed the following
poem in Rashi's honor, without doubt wrongfully so,
although Abraham Ibn Ezra never recoiled from contradictions.

A star hath arisen on the horizon of France and shineth
  afar.
Peaceful it came, with all its cortege, from Sinai and
  Zion.
. . . . The blind he enlightens, the thirsty delights with
  his honey-comb,
He whom men call Parshandata, the Torah's clear in-
  terpreter.
All doubts he solves, whose books are Israel's joy,
Who pierceth stout walls, and layeth bare the law's mys-
  terious sense.
For him the crown is destined, to him belongeth royal
  homage.

When one sees with what severity and injustice
Abraham Ibn Ezra treats the French commentator, one
may well doubt whether this enthusiastic eulogy sprang
from his pen, capricious though we know him to have
been. "The Talmud," he said, "has declared that the
Peshat must never lose its rights. But following generations gave the first place to Derash, as Rashi did, who
pursued this method in commenting upon the entire
Bible, though he believed he was using Peshat. In
his works there is not one rational explanation out of a
thousand." As I have said, Rashi and Ibn Ezra were
not fashioned to understand each other.[145] The commentaries of David Kimhi [146] contain no such sharp
criticisms. By birth Kimhi was a Provençal, by literary
tradition a Spaniard. He often turned Rashi's Biblical
commentaries to good account for himself. Sometimes
he did not mention Rashi by name, sometimes he referred to him openly.

A pompous eulogy of Rashi was written by Moses ben Nahman, or Nahmanides,[147] in the introduction to his commentary on the Pentateuch; and the body of the work shows that he constantly drew his inspiration from Rashi and ever had Rashi before his eyes. At the same time he also opposes Rashi, either because the free ways of the French rabbi shocked him, or because the Frenchman's naïve rationalism gave offense to his mysticism. In fact, it is known that Nahmanides is one of the first representatives of Kabbalistic exegesis, and his example contributed not a little toward bringing it into credit. Even the author of the *Zohar*—that Bible of the Kabbalah, which under cover of false authority exercised so lasting an influence upon Judaism—whether or not he was Moses of Leon (about 1250-1305) used for his exegesis the commentary of Rashi, without, of course, mentioning it by name, and sometimes he even reproduced it word for word. The Kabbalist exegete Bahya or Behaia ben Asher, of Saragossa, in his commentary on the Pentateuch (1291) cites Rashi as one of the principal representatives of Peshat—behold how far we have gotten from Ibn Ezra, and how Rashi is cleared of unjust contempt.

Although Nahmanides was wrongly held to have been the disciple of Judah Sir Leon, it was he who introduced into Spain the works and the method of French Talmudists, whom he possibly came to know through his masters. Thus the Spanish Talmudists, though they boasted such great leaders as Alfasi and Maimonides, nevertheless accepted also the heritage of the French academies. Rashi's influence is perceptible and acknowledged in the numerous Talmudic writings

of Solomon ben Adret,[148] and it is clearly manifest in the
commentary on Alfasi by Nissim Gerundi (about 1350),
who copies Rashi literally, at the same time developing
his thought, not infrequently over-elaborating it.   He
also refutes Rashi at times, but his refutation is often
wrong.   The man, however, who best represents the
fusion of Spanish and French Talmudism was assuredly
Asher ben Jehiel,[149] who, a native of the banks of the
Rhine, implanted in Spain the spirit of French Judaism, and in his abridgment of the Talmud united
Spanish tradition, whose principal representative was
Alfasi, with Franco-German tradition, whose uncontested leader was Rashi.

Since that time Talmudic activity, the creative force
of which seems to have been exhausted, has been under-
going a change of character.   Asher ben Jehiel, or, as
he has been called, Rosh, terminated an important
period of rabbinical literature, the period of the
Rishonim.   We have seen how during this period
Rashi's reputation, at first confined within the limits
of his native province, extended little by little, until it
spread over the surrounding countries, like the tree of
which Daniel speaks, "whose height reached unto the
heaven, and the sight thereof to all the earth; whose
leaves were fair, and the fruit thereof much" (Dan. iv.
20-21).

CHAPTER XII

FROM THE EXPULSION OF THE JEWS FROM FRANCE TO THE PRESENT TIME

It might be supposed that the Jews of France, chased from their fatherland, and so deprived of their schools, would have disappeared entirely from the scene of literary history, and that the intellectual works brought into being by their activity in the domains of Biblical exegesis and Talmudic jurisprudence would have been lost forever. Such was by no means the case. It has been made clear that the French school exerted influence outside of France from the twelfth to the fourteenth century, and we shall now see how the Jews of France, saving their literary treasures in the midst of the disturbances, carried their literature to foreign countries, to Piedmont and to Germany. When the Jews of Germany were expelled in turn, Poland became the centre of Judaism, and the literary tradition was thus maintained without interruption up to the present time. It is an unique example of continuity. The vitality of Judaism gained strength in the misfortunes that successively assailed it,

> Per damna, per caedes, ab ipso
> Ducit opes animumque ferro.

A large number of Jews exiled from France established themselves in the north of Italy, where they formed distinct communities faithful to the ancient traditions. Thus they propagated the works of the French rabbis. Rashi's commentaries and the ritual collections following his teachings were widely copied there, and of course, truncated and mutilated. They served both as the text-books of students and as the breviaries, so to speak, of scholars.

They also imposed themselves, as we have seen, upon the Spanish rabbis, who freely recognized the superiority of the Jews of France and Germany in regard to Talmudic schools. Isaac ben Sheshet [150] said, " From France goes forth the Law, and the word of God from Germany." Rashi's influence is apparent in the Talmudic writings of this rabbi, as well as in the works, both Talmudic and exegetic in character, of his successor Simon ben Zemah Duran, [151] and in the purely exegetic works of the celebrated Isaac Abrabanel (1437-1509), who salutes in Rashi " a father in the province of the Talmud." It was in the fifteenth century that some of the super-commentaries were made to Rashi's commentary on the Pentateuch. The most celebrated—and justly celebrated—is that of Elijah ben Abraham Mizrahi, a Hebrew scholar, mathematician, and philosopher, who lived in Turkey. His commentary, says Wogue, " is a master-piece of logic, keen-wittedness, and Talmudic learning."

However, as if the creative force of the Jews had been exhausted by a prolific period lasting several centuries, Rashi's commentaries were not productive of original works in a similar style. Accepted everywhere, they became the law everywhere, but they did not stimulate to fresh effort. Scholars followed him, as the poet said, in adoring his footsteps from afar.

For if his works had spent their impulse, his personality, on the other hand, became more and more popular. Legends sprang up ascribing to him the attributes of a saint and universal scholar, almost a magician.[152] He was venerated as the father of rabbinical literature. In certain German communities, he, together with a few other rabbis, is mentioned in the prayer recited in commemoration of the dead, and his name is followed by the formula, " who enlightened the eyes of the Captivity by his commentaries.'' Rashi's commentaries not only exercised profound influence upon the literary movement of the Jews, but also wove a strain into the destinies of the Jews of France and Germany. During this entire period of terror, the true middle ages of the Jews, for whom the horrors of the First Crusade, like a " disastrous twilight," did not draw to an end until the bright dawn of the French Revolution, the thing that sustained and animated them, that enabled them to bear pillage and exploitation, martyrdom and exile, was their unremitting study of the Bible and the Talmud. And how could they have become so passionately devoted to the reading of the two books, if Rashi had not given them the key, if he had not thus converted the books into a safeguard for the Jews, a lamp in the midst of darkness, a bright hope against alien persecutions?

Rashi's prestige then became so great that the principal Jewish communities claimed him as their own,[153] and high-standing families alleged that they were connected with him. It is known that the celebrated mystic Eleazar of Worms (1160-1230) is a descendant of his.

A certain Solomon Simḥah, of Troyes, in 1297 wrote a casuistic, ethical work in which he claims to belong to the fourth generation descended from Rashi beginning with Rashi's sons-in-law. The family of the French rabbi may be traced down to the thirteenth century. At that time mention is made of a Samuel ben Jacob, of Troyes, who lived in the south of France. And it is also from Rashi that the family Luria, or Loria, pretends to be descended, although the titles for its claim are not incontestably authentic. The name of Loria comes, not, as has been said, from the river Loire, but from a little city of Italy, and the family itself may have originated in Alsace. Its head, Solomon, son of Samuel Spira (about 1375), traced his connection with Rashi through his mother, a daughter of Mattathias Treves, one of the last French rabbis. The daughter of Solomon, Miriam (this name seems to have been frequent in Rashi's family), was, it appears, a scholar. It is certain that the family has produced illustrious offspring, among them Yosselmann of Rosheim (about 1554), the famous rabbi and defender of the Jews of the Empire; Elijah Loanz (about 1564-1616), wandering rabbi, Kabbalist, and commentator; Solomon Luria [134] (died in 1573 at Lublin), likewise a Kabbalist and Talmudist, but of the highest rank, on account of his bold thinking and sense of logic, who renewed the study of the Tossafists; and Jehiel Heilprin (about 1725), descended from Luria through his mother, author of a valuable and learned Jewish chronicle followed by an index of rabbis. He declared he had seen a genealogical table on which Rashi's name appeared establishing his descent from so remote an ancestor as Johanan ha-Sandlar and including Rashi in the steps.[155] This family, which was divided into two branches, the Heilprins and the Lurias, still counts among its members renowned scholars and estimable merchants.

As if the numberless copies of his commentaries had not sufficed to spread Rashi's popularity, the discovery of printing lent its aid in giving it the widest possible vogue. The commentary on the Pentateuch is the first Hebrew work of which the date of printing is known. The edition was published at Reggio at the beginning of 1475 by the printer Abraham ben Garton. Zunz reckoned that up to 1818 there were seventeen editions in which the commentary appeared alone, and one hundred and sixty in which it accompanied the text. Some modifications were introduced into the commentary either because of the severity of the censors or because of the prudence of the editors. Among the books that the Inquisition confiscated in 1753 in a small city of Italy, there were twenty-one Pentateuchs with Rashi's commentary.

All the printed editions of the Babylonian Talmud are accompanied by Rashi's commentaries in the inner column and by the Tossafot in the outer column.

Rashi's authority gained in weight more and more, and he became representative in ordinary, as it were, of Talmudic exegesis. This fact is made evident by a merely superficial survey of the work *Bet Yosef* (House of Joseph), which is, one may say, an index to rabbinical literature. Rashi is mentioned here on every page. He is the official commentator of the Talmudic text. The author of the *Bet Yosef,* the learned Talmudist and Kabbalist Joseph ben Ephraim Karo (born 1448, died

at Safed, Palestine, at 87 years of age), places Rashi's
Biblical commentary on the same plane as the Aramaic
translation of the Bible. He recommends that it be
read on the Sabbath, at the same time as the Pentateuch
and the Targum. Luria goes even further. According
to him, when the Targum and Rashi cannot be read at
the same time, preference should be given to Rashi,
since he is more easily understood, and renders the text
more intelligible.

Rashi's commentary, therefore, entered into the religious life of the Jews. It is chiefly the commentaries
on the Five Books of Moses and the Five *Megillot,* the
Scriptural books forming part of the synagogue liturgy,
that were widely circulated in print and were made the
basis of super-commentaries. The best of these are the
super-commentary of Simon Ashkenazi, a writer of the
seventeenth century, born in Frankfort and died at Jerusalem, and the clear, ingenious super-commentary of
Sabbataï ben Joseph Bass, printer and bibliographer,
born in 1641, died at Krotoszyn in 1718.

The other representatives of the French school of
exegetes have fallen into oblivion. Rashi alone survived,
and what saved him, I greatly fear, were the Halakic
and Haggadic elements pervading his commentary. An
editor who ventured to undertake the publication (in
1705) of the commentary on the Pentateuch by Samuel
ben Meïr,[156] complains in the preface that his contemporaries found in it nothing worth occupying their time.
Rashi's commentary was better adapted to the average
intellects and to the Talmudic culture of its readers.

Rashi's Talmudic commentary, also, was more generally studied than other commentaries, and gave a more

stimulating impulse to rabbinical literature. Teachers and masters racked their brains to discover in it unexpected difficulties, for the sake of solving them in the most ingenious fashion. This produced the kind of literature known as *Ḥiddushim*, Novellae, and *Dikdukim*, subtleties. A rabbi, for example, would set himself the task of counting the exact number of times the expression "that is to say" occurs in the commentary on the first three Talmudic treatises. Jacob ben Joshua Falk (died 1648), who believed Rashi had appeared to him in a dream, attempted in his "Defense of Solomon" to clear the master of all attacks made upon him. Solomon Luria and Samuel Edels (about 1555-1631), or, as is said in the schools, the Maharshal and the Maharsha, explain the difficult passages of Rashi's Talmudic commentary, sometimes by dint of subtlety, sometimes by happy corrections. Still more meritorious are the efforts of Joel Sirkes (died in 1640 at Cracow), who often skilfully altered Rashi's text for the better.

By a curious turn in affairs it was the Christians who in the province of exegesis took up the legacy bequeathed by Rashi. While grammar and exegesis by reason of neglect remained stationary among the Jews, the humanists cultivated them eagerly. Taste for the classical languages had aroused a lively interest in Hebrew and a desire to know the Scriptures in the original. The Reformation completed what the Renaissance had begun, and the Protestants placed the Hebrew Bible above the Vulgate. Rashi, it is true, did not gain immediately from this renewal of Biblical studies; greater inspiration was derived from the more methodical and more scientific Spaniards. But his eclipse was only momentary. Richard Simon, who gave so vigorous an impulse to Biblical studies in France, and who, if Bossuet had not forestalled him, would possibly have originated a scientific method of exegesis, profited by the commentaries of the man he called *major et prae-stantior theologus*. All the Christians with pretensions to Hebrew scholarship, who endeavored to understand the Bible in the original, studied Rashi, not only because he helped them to grasp the meaning of the text, but also because in their eyes he was the official rabbinical authority. He was quoted, abridged, and plagiarized— a clear sign of popularity. Soon the need arose to render him accessible to all theologians, and he was translated into the academic language, that is, into Latin. Partial translations appeared in great number between 1556 and 1710. Finally, J. F. Breithaupt made a complete translation, for which he had recourse to various manu-scripts. His work is marked by clear intelligence and great industry. This translation as well as the com-mentary of Nicholas de Lyra might still be consulted with profit by an editor of Rashi.

Since the Christians did not devote themselves to the Talmud as much as to the Bible, they made but little use of the Talmudic commentaries of the French rabbi. Nevertheless John Buxtorf the Elder, who calls Rashi *consummatissimus ille theologiae judaicae doctor,* frequently appeals to his authority in the " Hebrew and Chaldaic Lexicon." Other names might be mentioned besides Buxtorf's.

Nor did Rashi fail to receive the supreme honor of being censored by the Church. Under St. Louis *autos-da-fé* were made of his works, and later the Inquisition pursued them with its rigorous measures. They were prohibited in Spain and burnt in Italy. The ecclesiastical censors eliminated or corrected whatever seemed to them an attempt upon the dignity of religion. At the present time many French ecclesiastics know Rashi only for his alleged blasphemies against Christianity.

While the Catholics and Protestants who possessed Hebrew learning applied themselves to the study of Rashi, among the Jews

" he was always revered, always admired, even as an exegete, but he was admired to so high a degree that no one thought of continuing his work and of deepening the furrow he had so vigorously opened. It seemed as though his commentary had raised the Pillars of Hercules of Biblical knowledge and as though with him exegesis had said its last word. During this period the grammatical and rational study of the word of God fell into more and more neglect, and its real meaning became increasingly obscured. The place of a serious and sincere exegesis was taken by frivolous combinations, subtle comparisons, and mystical interpretations carried out according to preconceived notions and based on the slightest accident of form in the text. Rashi had many admirers, but few successors." [157]

Isaiah Horwitz (1570-1630), whose ritual and ethical collection is still very popular in Eastern Europe, compares Rashi's commentaries to the revelation on Sinai. " In every one of his phrases," he says, " marvellous things are concealed, for he wrote under Divine inspiration." His son Sabbataï Sheftel is even more striking in his expressions; he says, " I know by tradition that whoever finds a defect in Rashi, has a defect in his own brain." It was related that when Rashi was worried by some difficult question, he shut himself up in a room, where God appeared to throw light upon his doubts. The apparition came to him when he was plunged in profound sleep, and he did not return to his waking senses until some one brought him an article from the wall of his room. Thus a superstitious, sterile respect replaced the intelligent and productive admiration of the earlier centuries.

To revive the scientific spirit and the rational study of the Scriptures, a Moses Mendelssohn (1729-1786) was needed. With the year 1780, when his translation of the Pentateuch and his commentary upon it appeared, the renaissance of Jewish learning commenced; even the study of the Talmud, regenerated by the critical spirit of the time, was resumed. Mendelssohn himself drew largely upon Rashi's commentary, correcting the text when it seemed corrupt, trying to decipher the French *laazim,* and paying attention to the essential meaning of Rashi's explanations, either for the sake of completing or defending them, or for the sake of refuting them in the name of taste and good sense. His collaborators and disciples, the Biurists,—as they are called, after *Biur,* the general title of their works—desirous of reconciling the natural meaning of the text with the traditional interpretations, often turned to good account the views of the French commentator. These writings, which renewed the rational study of Hebrew and the taste for a sound exegesis, worthily crown the work begun by the rabbi of the eleventh century. At this day the Perush of Rashi and the Biur of Mendelssohn are the favorite commentaries of orthodox Jews.

Since Mendelssohn the glorious tradition of learning has not been interrupted again, and Rashi's work con-

tinues to be bound up with the destinies of Jewish
literature. The nineteenth century will make a place
for itself in the annals of this literature; for the love
of Jewish learning has inspired numerous scholars, and
the renown of most of them is connected with Rashi.
Zunz (1794-1886) became known in 1823 through his
essay on Rashi, a model of critical skill and learning,
despite inevitable mistakes and omissions. Geiger [158]
won a name for himself by his studies on the French
exegetic school. Heidenheim [159] wrote a work distinguished for subtlety, to defend the explanations of
Rashi from the grammatical point of view. Samuel
David Luzzatto (1800-1865), with his usual brilliancy,
made a warm defense of Rashi; and, finally, I. H.
Weiss [160] dedicated to him a study dealing with certain
definite points in Rashi's life and work. When Luzzatto
took up the defense of Rashi with ardor, it was to place
him over against Abraham Ibn Ezra, who, in Luzzatto's
opinion, was too highly exalted. The considerable
progress made by exegesis and philology rendered many
scholars aware of the defectiveness of Rashi's Biblical
commentaries; while Ibn Ezra was more pleasing to
them on account of his scientific intellect and his daring.
But the French commentator lost nothing of his authority in the eyes of the conservative students of Hebrew,
who continued to see in him an indispensable help.
This influence of Rashi's contains mixed elements of
good and evil. In some measure he created the fortune
of Midrashic exegesis, and he is in a slight degree
responsible for the relative stagnation of Biblical as
compared with Talmudic studies in Eastern Europe.

In Talmudic literature, on the contrary, Rashi's authority is uncontested, in fact, cannot be contested. Its stimulating impulse is not yet exhausted. While the Talmudists of the old school saw in him the official, consecrated guide, the Rapoports,[161] the Weisses, the Frankels,[162] all who cultivated the scientific and historic study of the Talmud, lay stress upon the excellence of his method and the sureness of his information. About twelve years ago, an editor wanted to publish the entire Talmud in one volume. He obtained the authorization of the rabbis only upon condition that he printed Rashi's commentary along with the text.

Thus Rashi's reputation has not diminished in the course of eight centuries. On the first of August, 1905, it was exactly eight hundred years that the eminent scholar died at Troyes. As is proper, the event was marked by a commemoration of a literary and scientific character. Articles on Rashi appeared in the Jewish journals and reviews. Such authorities as Dr. Berliner, Mr. W. Bacher, and others, sketched his portrait and published appreciations of his works. Dr. Berliner, moreover, issued a new edition of Rashi's Pentateuch Commentary in honor of the anniversary, and, as was mentioned above, Mr. S. Buber celebrated the occasion by inaugurating the publication of the hitherto unedited works of Rashi, beginning with the *Sefer ha-Orah.*

CONCLUSION

The beautiful unity of his life and the noble simplicity of his nature make Rashi's personality one of the most sympathetic in Jewish history. The writings he left are of various kinds and possess various interests for us. His Decisions and Responsa acquaint us with his personal traits, and with the character of his contemporaries; his religious poems betray the profound faith of his soul, and his sensitiveness to the woes of his brethren. But above all Rashi was a commentator. He carved himself a niche from which he has not been removed, and though his work as a commentator has been copied, it will doubtless remain impossible of absolute imitation. Rashi, then, is a commentator, though as such he cannot aspire to the glory of masters like Maimonides and Jehudah ha-Levi. But the task he set himself was to comment upon the Bible and the Talmud, the two living sources that feed the great stream of Judaism, and he fulfilled the task in a masterly fashion and conclusively. Moreover he touched upon nearly all branches of Jewish literature, grammar, exegesis, history, and archaeology. In short his commentaries became inseparable from the texts they explain. For, if in some respects his work despite all this may seem of secondary importance and inferior in creative force to the writings of a Saadia or a Maimonides, it gains enormously in value by the discussion and comment it evoked and the influence it exercised.

Rashi, one may say, is one of the fathers of rabbinical literature, which he stamped with the impress of his clear, orderly intellect. Of him it could be written: "With him began a new era for Judaism, the era of science united to profound piety."

His influence was not limited to scholarly circles. He is one of the rare writers who have had the privilege of becoming truly popular, and his renown was not tarnished, as that of Maimonides came near being on account of bitter controversies and violent contests. He was not the awe-inspiring master who is followed from afar; he was the master to whom one always listens, whose words are always read; and the writers who imitate his work—with more or less felicity—believe themselves inspired by him. The middle ages knew no Jewish names more famous than those of Jehudah ha-Levi and Maimonides; but how many nowadays read their writings and understand them wholly? The "Diwan" as well as the "Guide of the Perplexed" are products of Jewish culture grafted upon Arabic culture. They do not unqualifiedly correspond to present ideas and tastes. Rashi's work, on the contrary, is essentially and intimately Jewish. Judaism could renounce the study of the Bible and of that other Bible, the Talmud, only under penalty of intellectual suicide. And since, added to respect for these two monuments, is the difficulty of understanding them, the commentaries holding the key to them are assured of an existence as along as theirs.

Rashi's writings, therefore, extend beyond the range of merely occasional works, and his influence will not soon die out. His influence, indeed, is highly productive of results, since his commentaries do not arrest the march of science, as witness his disciples who enlarged and enriched the ground he had ploughed so vigorously, and whose fame only adds to the lustre of Rashi's name. The field he commanded was the entire Jewish culture of France—of France, which for a time he turned into the classic land of Biblical and Talmudic studies. "In him," says M. Israël Lévi, "is personified the Judaism of Northern France, with its scrupulous attachment to tradition, its naïve, untroubled faith, and its ardent piety, free from all mysticism." Nor was Rashi confined to France; his great personality dominated the whole of Judaism. Dr. M. Berliner writes: "Even nowadays, after eight hundred years have rolled by, it is from him we draw our inspiration,—we who cultivate the sacred literature,—it is his school to which we resort, it is his commentaries we study. These commentaries are and will remain our light in the principal department of our intellectual patrimony."

Doubtless Rashi is but a commentator, yet a commentator without peer by reason of his value and influence. And, possibly, this commentator represents most exactly, most powerfully, certain general propensities of the Jewish people and certain main tendencies of Jewish culture. Rashi, then, has a claim, universally recognized, upon a high place of honor in our history and in our literature.

APPENDIX I

THE FAMILY OF RASHI

APPENDIX I

THE FAMILY OF RASHI

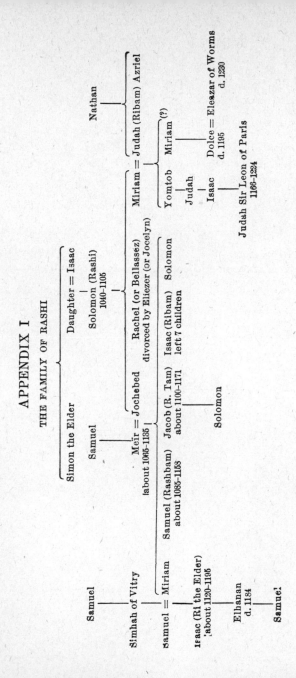

APPENDIX II

BIBLIOGRAPHY

APPENDIX II

BIBLIOGRAPHY

A. The Works of Rashi

A critical revision of Rashi's works remains to be made. They were used to such an extent, and, up to the time when printing gave definiteness to existing diversities, so many copies were made, that some of the works were preserved in bad shape, others were lost, and others again received successive additions.

1. BIBLICAL COMMENTARIES.—They cover nearly all the twenty-four books of the Bible.

Job.—"On *Job* the manuscripts are divided into series, according to whether or not they break off at xl. 28 of the text. The one series gives Rashi's commentary to the end; the other, on the ground that Rashi's death prevented him from finishing his work, completes the commentary with that of another rabbi, R. Jacob Nazir" (Arsène Darmesteter). Geiger attributes this supplementary commentary, which exists in several versions, to Samuel ben Meïr; others attribute it to Joseph Kara. Some regard it as a compilation; others, again, assert that the entire commentary was not written by Rashi.

Ezra and *Nehemiah.*—Some authors deny that Rashi composed commentaries on *Ezra* and *Nehemiah.*

Chronicles.—It is certain that the commentary on *Chronicles*, which does not occur in the good manuscripts, and which was published for the first time at Naples in 1487, is not to be ascribed to Rashi. This was observed by so early a writer as Azulaï, and it has been clearly demonstrated by Weiss (*Kerem Hemed*, v., 232 *et seq.*). It seems that Rashi did not comment upon *Chronicles* at all (in spite of Zunz and Weiss). Concerning the author of

the printed commentary there is doubt. According to Zunz
(*Zur Geschichte und Literatur*, p. 73), it must have been
composed at Narbonne about 1130-1140 by the disciples of
Saadia (?).

2. TALMUDIC COMMENTARIES.—Rashi did not comment on
the treatises lacking a Gemara, namely, *Eduyot*, *Middot*
(the commentary upon which was written by Shemaiah),
and *Tamid* (in the commentary on which Rashi is cited).
It is calculated that, in all, Rashi commented on thirty
treatises (compare Azulaï, *Shem ha-Gedolim*, s. v., Weiss,
and below, section B, 2).

Pesahim.—The commentary on *Pesahim* from 99*b* on is
the work of Rashbam.

Taanit.—So early a writer as Emden denied to Rashi the
authorship of the commentary on *Taanit;* and his conclusions are borne out by the style. There was a commentary
on *Taanit* cited by the Tossafot, which forms the basis of
the present commentary; and this may have belonged to
the school of Rashi.

Moëd Katan.—The commentary on *Moëd Katan* is attributed by Reifmann to Gershom (*Monatsschrift*, III). According to B. Zomber (Rashi's Commentary on *Nedarim*
and *Moëd Katan*, Berlin, 1867), who shows that Gershom's
commentary is different, the extant commentary is a first
trial of Rashi's and was later recast by him. This would
explain the differences between the commentary under consideration and the one joined to the *En Jacob* and to Rif,
which is more complete and might be the true commentary
by Rashi. These conclusions have been attacked by Rabbinowicz (*Dikduke Soferim*, II), who accepts Reifmann's
thesis. Zomber replied in the *Moreh Derek*, Lyck, 1870; and
Rabbinowicz in turn replied in the *Moreh ha-Moreh*, Munich,
1871. To sum up, both sides agree in saying that the basis
of the present commentary was modified by Rashi or by
some one else. According to I. H. Weiss various versions of
Rashi's Commentary were current. The most incomplete
is the present one. That accompanying Rif is more complete, though also not without faults.

Nedarim.—The commentary on *Nedarim*, from 22*b* to 25*b*, may contain a fragment by R. Gershom. Nor, to judge from the style, does the remainder seem to belong to Rashi. Good writers do not cite it. Reifmann attributes it to Isaiah da Trani, Zomber to the disciples of Rashi.

Nazir.—Several critics deny to Rashi the authorship of the commentary on *Nazir.* Although there are no strong reasons for so doing, the doubt exists; for differences are pointed out between this and the other commentaries. P. Chajes holds that Rashi's disciples are responsible for the commentaries on *Nedarim* and *Taanit.*

Zebahim.—The commentary on *Zebahim* is corrupt and has undergone interpolations; but there are no strong reasons why it should not be ascribed to Rashi.

Baba Batra.—Rashbam completed his grandfather's commentary on *Baba Batra* from 29*a* on, or, rather, later writers supplemented Rashi's commentary with that of his grandson. This supplement is to be found at the Bodleian in a more abridged and, without doubt, in a more authentic form.

Makkot.—The commentary on *Makkot*, from 19*b* on, was composed by Judah ben Nathan (see note in the editions). It seems that a commentary on the whole by Rashi was known to Yomtob ben Abraham.

Horaïot.—The commentary on *Horaïot* was not written by Rashi (Reifmann, *Ha-Maggid* xxi. 47-49).

Meïlah.—It is more certain that the commentary on *Meïlah* was not written by Rashi. Numerous errors and additions have been pointed out. According to a manuscript of Halberstamm it would belong to Judah ben Nathan.

Keritot and *Bekorot.*—The commentary on *Keritot* is not Rashi's, and that on *Bekorot*, after 57*b*, according to Bezalel Ashkenazi, is also not Rashi's.

3. PIRKE ABOT.—The commentary on the *Pirke Abot*, printed for the first time at Mentone in 1560, was cited by Simon ben Zemah Duran (d. 1444) as being by Rashi. But Jacob Emden (d. 1776) denies Rashi's authorship, and

justly so. One manuscript attributes the commentary to Isaiah da Trani, another to Kimhi. Though the numerous copies present differences, it is not impossible that they are derived from a common source, which might be Rashi's commentary; for despite some diffuseness in certain passages, the present commentary is in his style. The Italian *laazim* may have been made by Italian copyists.

4. BERESHIT RABBAH.—The commentary on *Bereshit Rabbah*. According to A. Epstein (*Magazin* of Berliner, xiv. *Ha-Hoker* I), this commentary, incorrectly printed (the first time at Venice, 1568), is composed of two different commentaries. The basis of the first is the commentary of Kalonymos ben Sabbataï, of Rome; the second is anonymous and of later date. A third commentary exists in manuscript, and is possibly of the school of Rashi.

Mention should be made of a commentary on the Thirty-two Rules by R. José ha-Gelili, attributed to Rashi and published in the *Yeshurun* of Kobak.

5. RESPONSA.—The *Responsa* of Rashi have not been gathered together into one collection. Some Responsa mixed with some of his decisions occur in the compilations already cited and in the following Halakic compilations: *Eben ha-Ezer* by Eliezer ben Nathan (Prague, 1670), *Or Zarua* by Isaac ben Moses of Vienna (I-II, Zhitomir, 1862; III-V, Jerusalem, 1887), *Shibbole ha-Leket* by Zedekiah ben Abraham Anaw (Wilna, 1887, ed. Buber), *Mordecai*, by Mordecai ben Hillel (printed together with Rif), *Responsa* by Meïr of Rothenburg (Cremona, 1557; Prague, 1608; Lemberg, 1860; Berlin, 1891-92; Budapest, 1896), etc. (see below, section B, and Buber, Introd. to *Sefer ha-Orah*, pp. 152 *et seq.*

6. In rabbinical literature we find quotations from Responsa collections bearing upon special points in Talmudic law, such as ablutions, the making and the use of *Tefillin*, the *Zizit*, the order of the *Parashiot*, the blessing of the priests, the ceremony of the Passover eve, the slaughter of animals, the case of diseased animals, impurity in women, etc.

7. These collections have penetrated in part into the
SEFER HA-PARDES, the MAHZOR VITRY, and the other compilations mentioned in chap. IX. Upon this point see chap. IX
and articles by A. Epstein and S. Poznanski published in
the *Monatsschrift*, xli.

8. THE LITURGICAL POEMS by Rashi, some of which are
printed in the collections of Selihot of the German ritual,
are enumerated by Zunz in *Synagogale Poesie des Mittel-
alters*, Berlin, 1865, pp. 252-4.

Three books have been wrongly attributed to Rashi: a
medical work, *Sefer ha-Refuah;* a grammatical work, *Le-
shon Limmudim*, actually composed by Solomon ben Abba
Mari of Lunel; and an entirely fanciful production called
Sefer ha-Pardes (incorrect for *Sefer ha-Parnas*).

B. THE EDITIONS OF RASHI'S WORKS

1. THE BIBLICAL COMMENTARIES I.—According to A. Darmesteter "twenty different editions have been counted of
Rashi's commentary, complete or partial, without the Hebrew text. As for the editions containing the Bible
together with Rashi's commentary, their number amounts
to seventeen complete editions and 155 partial editions, of
the latter of which 114 are for the Pentateuch alone."
The list of these editions is to be found in Fürst, *Biblio-
theca judaica* (Leipsic, 1849, 2d vol. 1851), II, pp. 78 *et
seq.;* Steinschneider, *Catalogue of the Hebrew Books in the
Bodleian Library* (Berlin, 1852-1860), col. 2340-57; Ben
Jakob, *Ozar ha-Sefarim* (Wilna, 1887), pp. 629 *et seq.* The
first two works enumerate also the super-commentaries on
Rashi.

II. *Latin Translations.*—Besides numerous partial translations, also listed in the works of Fürst and Steinschneider, a complete translation exists by J. F. Breithaupt,
Gotha, 1710 (Pentateuch) and 1713-1714 (Prophets and
Hagiographa) in quarto.

III. *German Translations.*—L. Haymann, *R. Solomon
Iarchi, Ausführlicher Commentar über den Pentateuch.*
1st vol., Genesis, Bonn, 1883, in German characters and

without the Hebrew text. Leopold Dukes, *Rashi zum Pentateuch*, Prague, 1833-1838, in Hebrew characters and with the Hebrew text opposite. J. Dessauer, a translation into Judæo-German with a vowelled text, Budapest, 1863. Some fragmentary translations into Judæo-German had appeared before, by Broesch, in 1560, etc.

2. THE TALMUDIC COMMENTARIES.—All the editions of the Talmud contain Rashi's commentary. Up to the present time forty-five complete editions of the Talmud have been counted.

3. RESPONSA.—Some Responsa addressed to the rabbis of Auxerre were published by A. Geiger, *Melo Hofnaim*, Berlin, 1840. Twenty-eight Responsa were edited by B. Goldberg, *Hofes Matmonim*, Berlin, 1845, thirty by J. Müller, *Réponses faites par de célèbres rabbins français et lorrains des xie et xiie siècles*, Vienna, 1881. Some isolated Responsa were published in the collection of Responsa of Judah ben Asher (50*a*, 52*b*), Berlin, 1846, in the *Ozar Nehmad* II, 174, in *Bet-Talmud* II, pp. 296 and 341, at the end of the study on Rashi cited below in section C, etc.

4. THE SEFER HA-PARDES was printed at Constantinople in 1802 according to a defective copy. The editor intercalated fragments of the *Sefer ha-Orah*, which he took from an often illegible manuscript.

THE MAHZOR VITRY, the existence of which was revealed by Luzzatto, was published according to a defective manuscript of the British Museum, under the auspices of the literary Society *Mekize Nirdamim*, by S. Hurwitz, Berlin, 1890-1893, 8°.

C. CRITICAL WORKS OF REFERENCE

Book I. Chap. I.—On the situation of the Jews in France in general, the following works may be read with profit:

Zunz, *Zur Geschichte und Literatur*, Berlin, 1845.

Güdemann, *Geschichte des Erziehungswesens und der Cultur der Juden in Frankreich und Deutschland*, Vienna, 1880, 8° (Hebrew translation by Friedberg under the title *Ha-Torah weha-Hayim*, ed. Achiassaf, Warsaw, 1896).

Berliner, *Aus dem Leben der deutschen Juden im Mittelalter*, Berlin, 1900.

Abrahams, *Jewish Life in the Middle Ages*, Jewish Publication Society of America, Philadelphia, 1896. Concerning Gershom ben Judah, see Gross, *Gallia judaica*, Paris, 1897, pp. 299 *et seq.*

Chap. II-IV.—Works in general. Besides the accounts of Rashi in the works of the historians of the Jewish people and literature (especially Graetz, *Geschichte der Juden*, Leipsic, 1861, vol. vi; English translation published by the Jewish Publication Society of America, Philadelphia, 1895, vols. iii and iv; Hebrew translation by L. Rabbinovitch, Warsaw, 1894, vol. iv), there are two most important studies of Rashi:

1. Zunz, *Salomon ben Isaac, genannt Raschi*, in Zunz's *Zeitschrift für die Wissenschaft des Judenthums*, 1823, pp. 277-384. Additions by Zunz himself in the preface to *Gottesdienstliche Vorträge*, and in the catalogue of the library at Leipsic, by Berliner in the *Monatsschrift* xi and xii, by Klein, *ibid.* xi. One appreciates the originality of this study all the more if one reads in the *Histoire littéraire de la France*, xvi., the passage in which are collected all the legends retailed concerning Rashi in the world of Christian scholars at the time when Zunz wrote.

Zunz's essay was translated into Hebrew and enriched with notes by Samson Bloch, *Vita R. Salomon Isaki*, Lemberg 1840, 8°. Second edition by Hirschenthal, Warsaw, 1862. The essay was abridged by Samuel Cahen in the *Journal de l'Institut historique*, I, and plagiarized by the Abbé Etienne Georges, *Le rabbin Salomon Raschi* (sic) in the *Annuaire administratif* . . . . *du département de l'Aube*, 1868. *Compare* Clement-Mullet, *Documents pour servir à l'histoire du rabbin Salomon fils de Isaac* in the *Mémoires de la Societé d'Agriculture* . . . . *de l'Aube*, xix.

2. I. H. Weiss, *R. Salomon bar Isaac* (in Hebrew), in the *Bet Talmud* II, 1881-82, Nos. 2-10 (cf. iii. 81). Off-print under the title *Biographien jüdischer Gelehrten*, 2nd leaflet, Vienna, 1882.

Other works on Rashi are: M. H. Friedlaender, *Raschi*, in *Jüdisches Litteraturblatt*, xvii. M. Grünwald, *Raschi's Leben und Wirken*, *ibid.* x.

Concerning the date of Rashi's death, see Luzzatto, in the *Orient*, vii. 418.

Book II. Chap. V.—Concerning the *laazim* see A. Darmesteter in the *Romania* I. (1882), and various other essays reprinted in the *Reliques scientifiques*, Paris, 1890, vol. i. The deciphering of the *laazim* by Berliner in his edition of the commentary on the Pentateuch is defective, and that of Landau in his edition of the Talmud (Prague, 1829; 2d ed., 1839) is still more inadequate. A. Darmesteter's essay on the *laazim* of all the Biblical commentaries will soon appear.

Chap. VI.—On Moses ha-Darshan there is a monograph by A. Epstein, Vienna 1891; and on Menahem ben Helbo one by S. Poznanski, Warsaw, 1904.

Concerning the Biblical commentaries see..

A. Geiger, *Nite Naamanim, oder Sammlung aus alten schätzbaren Manuscripten*, Berlin, 1847.

Parshandata, die Nordfranzösische Exegetenschule, Leipsic, 1855.

Antoine Lévy, *Die Exegese bei den französischen Juden vom 10 bis 14 Jahrhundert* (translated from the French), Leipsic, 1873.

Nehemiah Kronberg, *Raschi als Exeget* . . . , Halle [1882]. In Winter und Wünsche, *Die jüdische Litteratur*, ii, Berlin, 1897, *Die Bibelexegese*, by W. Bacher.

Chap. VII.—See especially the above mentioned essay of Weiss, and by the same author, *Dor Dor we-Dorschaw, Zur Geschichte der jüdischen Tradition*, Vienna, iv, 1887.

In Winter und Wünsche *ibid.* ii, *Die Halacha in Italien, Frankreich und Deutschland*, by A. Kaminka.

Chap. VIII.—A. Berliner, *Zur Charakteristik Raschi's* in *Gedenkbuch zur Erinnerung an D. Kaufmann* (published also separately), Breslau, 1900.

Chap. IX.—Weiss, *ibid.;* Epstein in the *Monatsschrift*, xli.

Chap. X.—Zunz, *Die Synagogale Poesie*, Berlin, 1855.
Clément-Mullet, *Poésies ou Selichot attribuées à Raschi*, in
the *Mémoires de la Société académique de l'Aube*, xx; published by itself, Troyes, 1856.

Book III. Chaps. XI-XII.—The history of Rashi's influence forms part of the general history of later rabbinical
literature. Mention, therefore, may be made of the following works, besides the history of Graetz, the works of Geiger and of A. Lévy, and the references in Winter und
Wünsche, II:

Zunz, *Zur Geschichte und Literatur*.

Renan [and Neubauer], *Les rabbins français (Histoire
littéraire de la France)*, Paris, 1877.

L. Wogue, *Histoire de la Bible et de l'exégèse biblique*,
Paris, 1881.

I. H. Weiss, *Dor Dor we-Dorshaw*, iv and v.

Gross, *Gallia judaica*, Paris, 1897, *passim*.

Berliner, *Beiträge zur Geschichte der Raschi-Commen-
tare*, Berlin, 1903.

It is impossible to enumerate all the monographs and all
the magazine articles. Concerning Samuel b. Meïr, see
Rosin, *R. Samuel ben Meïr als Schrifterklärer*, Breslau,
1880; concerning Jacob Tam, see Weiss, *Rabbenu Tam*, in
the *Bet Talmud*, iii; concerning Jacob b. Simson, see
Epstein in the *Revue des études juives*, xxxv, pp. 240 *et seq.;*
concerning Shemaiah, see A. Epstein in the *Monatsschrift*,
xli, pp. 257, 296, 564; concerning Simson b. Abraham, see
H. Gross in the *Revue des études juives*, vii and viii; concerning Judah Sir Leon, see Gross in Berliner's *Magazin*,
iv and v.

The influence of Rashi upon Nicholas de Lyra and Luther
is the subject of an essay by Siegfried in *Archiv für wis-
senschaftliche Erforschung des Alten Testaments*, i and ii.
For Nicholas de Lyra alone, see Neumann in the *Revue des
études juives*, xxvi and xxvii.

Concerning Rashi's descendants, see Epstein, *Mishpaḥat
Luria et Kohen-Zedek* in *Ha-Goren*, i, Appendix.

NOTES

NOTES

[1] See W. Bacher, *Raschi und Maimuni, Monatsschrift*, XLIX, pp 1 *et seq.* Also D. Yellin and I. Abrahams, *Maimonides*. Philadelphia: The Jewish Publication Society of America, 1903.

[2] A legend has it that Vespasian made some Jews embark on three vessels, which were then abandoned on the open sea. One of the ships reached Arles, another Lyons, and the third Bordeaux. See Gross, *Gallia judaica*, p. 74.

[3] See, for example, p. 164.

[4] See Note 10.

[5] Israël Lévi.

[6] Théodor Reinach, *La Grande Encyclopédie, s. v.* Juifs.

[7] However, there had been Talmudists in France before this period.

[8] In the first quarter of the eleventh century Burchard, bishop of Worms, wrote the famous compilation which became one of the sources of canonical law. Concerning Lorraine, its Jews and Talmudical schools, see chap. II, p. 46 *et seq.*

[9] Not, as has been said with more ingenuity than verity, from Rosh Shibte Iehudah, chief of the tribes of Judah. Others, transposing the letters of "Rashi," called him *Yashar,* "the Just." He himself signed his name Solomon bar (not ben) Isaac, or Berabi Isaac. Once he wrote his signature Solomon of Troyes.

[10] Since "lune," moon, in Hebrew "yerah," is contained in "Lunel," a number of scholars coming from Lunel bore the surname "Yarhi." The city, in fact, is sometimes called "Jericho," as a result of that system of geographical nomenclature to which we owe the name "Kiryat Yeärim" for Nîmes (derived from the Latin *nemus*), and "Har" for Montpellier, etc. Through an analogy, based not so

much upon the significance of the words as upon a sort of assonance, Spain, France, and Britain in rabbinical litera- ture received the Hebrew names of Sefarad, Zarfat, and Rifat. Likewise the city of Dreux is called Darom, and so on.

[11] A spurious Rashi genealogy from Johanan ha-Sandlar was worked out in Italy at the end of the seventeenth cen- tury. In Appendix I is given a table of the connections and immediate descendants of Rashi. In chap. XII, p. 212 *et seq.* there are references concerning some of his later and more doubtful descendants.

[12] For this passage, see p. 112.

[13] See pp. 61-2. Also Berliner, *Aus dem Leben der deut- schen Juden.* The data that follow are taken from the *Kolbo,* the *Mahzor Vitry,* and other sources cited by Zunz, *Zur Geschichte,* pp. 167 *et seq.*

[14] See p. 81.

[15] See Epstein, *Die nach Raschi genannten Gebäude in Worms.*

[16] This is the epoch which marks the arrival of Jews in Great Britain. They went there, it seems, in the suite of William the Conqueror (1066). They always remained in touch with their co-religionists on the Continent, and were sometimes called by these "the Jews of the Island." For a while they enjoyed great prosperity, which, joined to their religious propaganda, drew upon them the hatred of the clergy. Massacred in 1190, exploited and utterly ruined in the thirteenth century, they were finally exiled in 1290.

[17] See p. 39.

[18] Surnamed "Segan Leviya," supposed—doubtless incor- rectly—to have come originally from Vitry in Champagne. He was a very conscientious pupil of Eliezer the Great. Died about 1070.

[19] He is the author of the famous Aramaic poem read at the Pentecost, beginning with the words *Akdamot Millin.* He must not be confounded with his contemporary of the same name, Meïr ben Isaac (of Orleans?), to whom also some liturgic poems are attributed. Another rabbi of Or-

leans, Isaac ben Menahem (according to Gross, *Gallia
judaica*, pp. 32-3, probably the father of Meïr), was older
than Rashi, who quotes some of his Talmudic explanations,
and some of the notes written on his copy of the Talmud.
There is nothing to prove, as Gross maintains, that Rashi
was his pupil. It is not even certain that he knew him
personally.

[20] See p. 77 for Rashi's relations to his teachers.

[21] A Responsum signed by Rashi shows that he was the
tutor of the children of a certain Joseph, whose father had
been administrator of the community.

[22] For a long time it was thought and said that once when
Rashi was sick, he dictated a Responsum to his daughter.
As Zunz was the first to show, this story about Rashi's sec-
retary is based upon the faulty reading of a text. Another
legend proved false! Science is remorseless. See *Sefer ha-
Pardes*, ed. Constantinople, 33*d*, where one must read, ולבן בת
not ולכן בתי. See Zunz, *Zur Geschichte*, p. 567, and Berliner, *Hebräische Bibliographie*, XI; also, *Monatsschrift*,
XXI.

[23] As has been shown (chap. II, p. 51) Rashi may have
begun to write commentaries upon the Talmud during his
sojourn in Lorraine. However that may be, it is difficult
to distinguish in this huge production between the work of
his youth and that of his maturity or old age.

[24] That is to say " very beautiful." It is a name frequently
borne by French Jewesses in the middle ages. Some give
the name of her husband as Ephraim. In chap. XI, pp. 187
et seq. the sons-in-law and grandchildren of Rashi will
receive further consideration. See also Appendix I.

[25] According to Jacob Molin ha-Levi, called Maharil,
rabbi of Mayence, later of Worms, where he died in 1427.
Christian marriages bore many points of resemblance to
Jewish marriages. See the work of Lecoy de la Marche,
La chaire française au moyen-âge.

[26] See pp. 165-6.

[27] The economic influence of the Crusades has also been
exaggerated. The Crusaders in Palestine came into rela-

tions with scarcely any other Turks than those but slightly civilized, and thus saw little of the brilliant Arabic civilization. The Jews certainly contributed more than the Crusades to the development of commerce and the increase of wealth.

[28] According to a less popular form of the legend, Godfrey of Bouillon disguised himself as a beggar, and obtained entrance into Rashi's home by asking for alms. But the night before, the visit of the lord had been announced to Rashi in a dream, and on his approach Rashi arose and hailed him by the title of hero. It was in this way that Joan of Arc recognized Charles VII lost in the crowd of his courtiers.

[29] See chap. VIII, pp. 164 *et seq.* for further details. The same chapter throws more light on Rashi's spiritual nature.

[30] Concerning this enigmatical kinsman of Rashi, see chap. XI, pp. 186-7.

[31] See chap. VI, p. 125.

[32] The mistake arises from the fact that certain cursive writing is called "Rashi script." It was generally employed in copying rabbinical works, among others, the works of Rashi. The term indicates the wide popularity enjoyed by the works of Rashi.

[33] See p. 45.

[34] See chap. VI, p. 105.

[35] The *Megillat Taanit* is a collection of ephemerides or calendars, indicating the days on which happy events occurred, and on which it is forbidden to fast. The little work, written in Aramaic, but enlarged by Hebrew glosses, is attributed by the Talmud to Hananiah ben Hezekiah ben Garon, or Gorion (first century); the nucleus about which the book was built up seems to go back as far as Maccabean times.

[36] See Note 94.

[37] Collection of texts not incorporated in the Mishnah, the order of which is followed, now to explain it, now to complement it, and sometimes to contradict it. The redaction of the Tosefta is attributed to R. Ḥiyyah bar Abba (third century).

[38] When the aim of the Midrash is to interpret the legal and ritual portions of the Pentateuch, it is called Halakic; it is Haggadic when its aim is to interpret the narrative and moral portions (see chap. VI, p. 107). The Halakic Midrashim nevertheless contain much Haggadah. The redaction of the Mekilta, the commentary on Exodus, is attributed to R. Ishmael; that of the Sifra, or Torat Kohanim, the commentary on Leviticus, to R. Judah ben Ilaï; that of the Sifre, the commentary on Numbers and Deuteronomy, to R. Simon ben Yohaï and to the school of Rab, all scholars of the second and third centuries. The Sifra that Rashi employed was more complete than the one now available, and he cites a second Sifre, at present unknown.

[39] The Midrash Rabba, or Rabbot, consists of Haggadic compilations on the Pentateuch and the Five Rolls; the elements of this Midrash are comparatively ancient, but its definite redaction without doubt does not go farther back than the eighth century. Rashi did not know those portions of the Midrash Rabba which explain the Books of Exodus and Numbers.

[40] By this name are designated Haggadic collections for various distinguished times and seasons of the year. There are two Pesiktas, the Pesikta attributed to R. Kahana, a Babylonian Talmudist, though its redaction falls in the seventh century, and the Pesikta Rabbati, or Great Pesikta, doubtless compiled in Southern Italy in the ninth century. Rashi knew the first of these collections; and his citations aided Zunz in the reconstruction he made of this Midrash before the discovery of a manuscript by Buber confirmed his clear-sighted suppositions.

[41] Name of a Midrash on the Pentateuch, redacted by the pupils of R. Tanhuma. Quite recently the endeavor was made to prove that Rashi did not know the Tanhuma either in the current text or in the more extended text published by Buber in 1885, and that he called Tanhuma the Midrash Yelamdenu, which is lost, and which is said to be the prototype of the two versions of the Tanhuma. See Grünhut, in *Festschrift Berliner*, pp. 156-63.

[42] A Midrashic compilation, partly mystic in character, of the eighth century, but attributed to the Tanna R. Eliezer ben Hyrkanos the Great.

[43] Collection in three " gates," relating to history, especially to Biblical chronology. Its redaction is commonly attributed to R. José ben Halafta (second century).

[44] Sherira bar Hananiah, Gaon of Pumbedita, about 930-1000, a scholar of great activity, who left Responsa. The one bearing upon the chronology of the Talmudic and Gaonic periods is the chief source for the history of those times.

[45] Haï Gaon, born about 940, collaborator, then successor, of his father. He wrote much, and his reputation reached Europe. Philosopher, scholar, didactic poet, and commentator of the Bible, he left authoritative Responsa, Talmudic commentaries, collections of rabbinical jurisprudence, and a Hebrew dictionary, which has been lost.

[46] Aha or Ahaï of Shabha wrote, about 760, one hundred and ninety-one *Sheeltot* (Questions), casuistic homilies, connected with the Five Books of Moses.

[47] Yehudaï bar Nahman, Gaon of Sura (about 759 or 762), eminent Talmudist and adversary of the Karaites. He wrote Responsa and possibly the Halakot, a collection of legal and ritual rules. He is said to have been blind.

[48] Isaac Abrabanel was possibly the only Jew who unmasked Josephus and revealed his lies and flatteries. Judah Sir Leon (see chap. XI, p. 194) recognized that Kalir was not identical with the Tanna Eleazar ben Simon.

[49] Of Tahort, Northern Africa. He lived at the end of the ninth century and the beginning of the tenth.

[50] See chap. VI, p. 127 and Note 91.

[51] Exception can scarcely be made in favor of the preamble to the Song of Songs and the shorter one to Zechariah. In the one he briefly characterizes the Haggadic method; in the other he speaks of the visions of Zechariah, which, he says, are as obscure as dreams.

[52] At the end of the gloss the explanations of Menahem ben Saruk and Dunash ben Labrat are reproduced. This is

without doubt a later addition. For these two Spanish grammarians, see Note 91.

[53] Evidently it was not Rashi who commented on the work of Alfasi, his contemporary. It was a German Jew, who abridged the commentary of the French rabbi in order to make it harmonize with the work of the illustrious Spanish Talmudist. For several treatises the German Jew had more authentic texts than are now available. He sometimes cites Rashi by name. See J. Perles, *Die Berner Handschrift des kleinen Aruch*, in *Jubelschrift Graetz*, 1887.

[54] See Note 53.

[55] The Gallo-Roman dialects are divided into two groups, the dialects of the langue d'oc (southern) and those of the langue d'oïl (northern). It was Dante who introduced this somewhat irrational distinction based upon the different ways of saying "yes," that is, *oc* and *oïl* (Latin, *hoc* and *ille*).

[56] In the middle of the eleventh century, it must be added, differences between neighboring dialects were not yet very pronounced.

[57] James Darmesteter, Introduction to the *Reliques scientifiques*, of his brother Arsène Darmesteter (Paris, 1890), vol. I, p. XVIII.

[58] Eliezer ben Nathan, of Mayence (about 1145), correspondent of Meïr and of his sons Samuel and Jacob, author of the work *Eben ha-Ezer*, whence the passage quoted has been taken (§ 107, p. 36*a*).

[59] The Persian word *Parshandata*, name of one of the sons of Haman, was divided into *Parshan* and *data*, " expounder of the Law." This epithet is applied to Rashi in the poem attributed to Ibn Ezra, cited in chap. XI, p. 207.

[60] Rashi seems also to have known about the Targum of the Pseudo-Jonathan upon the Pentateuch. See Note 72.

[61] Concerning the development of Biblical studies in general, among Jews as well as Christians, see pp. 127 *et seq.*

[62] L. Wogue, *Histoire de la Bible et de l'exégèse biblique*, p. 250.

[63] See p. 38. This Midrash is taken from the Tanhuma.

[64] Psalms cxi. 6. Rashi cites the Biblical verses themselves, often only in part; but he did not know the division of the Bible into chapters and verses, which was made at a later day and was of Christian origin. Sometimes Rashi cites a verse by indicating the weekly lesson in which it occurs, or by giving the paragraph a title drawn from its contents, or from the name of the hero of the narrative.

[65] Proverbs viii. 22.

[66] Jeremiah ii. 3.

[67] The rule, however, has exceptions. Even according to Rashi's opinion, the word is in the absolute in Deut. xxxiii. 21 and Is. xlvi. 10. It is true that strictly speaking one might say the exceptions are only apparent.

[68] "We will praise and we will celebrate."

[69] For the meaning of this expression, see p. 107. The source here is still the Talmudic treatise Sanhedrin 91b.

[70] Rashi here cites Is. xiv. 25, inaccurately.

[71] Here Rashi might have cited also I Kings xii. 17.

[72] This interpretation, taken without doubt from Pseudo-Jonathan (see Note 60), explains the demonstrative pronoun. What follows is taken from the Mekilta (see Note 38).

[73] In fact the Targum translates it, "I will build Him a temple."

[74] Still according to the Mekilta. The Song of Songs is often applied by Jewish exegetes to the events of the Exodus from Egypt.

[75] The French laaz is corrupted in the editions. The reading should be פרי שנ״ט.

[76] Name of the last portion of Exodus. Rashi alludes to Ex. xxxviii. 27.

[77] Without doubt the murex, which gives the purple dye. The details are taken from the Talmud (treatise Menaḥot 44a at the top).

[78] A fantastic bit of etymology taken from the Talmud.

[79] Ex. xxvii. 20.

[80] Next to last portion of Exodus (xxx. 22 et seq.).

[81] Portion preceding next to last of Exodus.

[82] Ex. xxviii. 6.

[83] *Ib.* and 15. The first of these passages is noteworthy, Rashi says about it: "If I tried to explain how these two objects are made according to the text, the explanation would be fragmentary, and the reader would not get an idea of the whole. So I will first give a complete description of them, to which the reader can refer. After that I will explain the text verse by verse. The ephod resembles the robe worn by the Amazons," etc.

[84] L. Wogue.

[85] This is a distinction made in Hebrew but not rendered in the English version.

[86] I Sam. xxiii. 14.

[87] And not "shadow of death," which is etymologically impossible, though it is a rendition employed by most commentators.

[88] See Note 91.

[89] Collection of Midrashim long attributed to Simon Kara, father of a disciple of Rashi. This valuable compilation, which deals with the entire Bible, dates without doubt from the first half of the thirteenth century. An unsuccessful attempt has been made to prove that Rashi knew the *Yalkut.* His silence shows, on the contrary, that it was a later work. The Simon (sometimes Simson) whom he quotes is not the author of the *Yalkut.*

[90] Commentary on Gen. xxxvii. 1.

[91] Menahem ben Saruk, of Tortosa, lived at Cordova about 960 with the celebrated minister and Maecenas, the Jew Hasdaï Ibn Shaprut. He was the author of the *Mahberet*, one of the first complete lexicons of the Biblical language, full of interesting grammatical digressions.

His rival, Dunash ben Labrat, born at Fez, was both poet and grammarian. He wrote "Refutations" against Menahem, in rhyme and prose, which were full of impassioned criticisms and abundantly displayed fresh, correct insight. The polemics of these two scholars were continued by their disciples and were ended by Jacob Tam, Rashi's grandson.

[92] Abul-Walid Merwan ibn Janah (among the Jews, R.

Jonah), the most eminent representative of the Spanish
school, born at Cordova about 985; he studied at Lucena,
and died at Saragossa about 1050. Besides small polemic
works, he left a long one, "The Book of Detailed Re-
search," including a grammar and a dictionary. Ibn
Janaḥ was an original and profound grammarian. Unfortunately his disciples in popularizing weakened him.

Judah ben David (Abu Zakaria Yaḥia ibn Daūd) Hayyuj, who may be looked upon as the master of Janaḥ,
was originally from Fez but lived for the greater time at
Cordova (end of the tenth and beginning of the eleventh
century). He inspired remarkable disciples, among others
the statesman Samuel ha-Naggid Ibn Nagdela. He was the
first to discover the triliteral character of all Hebrew roots.

⁹³ Abraham ben Meïr Ibn Ezra (1092-1167), born at Toledo,
died at Rome. He left Spain in about his fortieth year,
and travelled through Europe, reaching also Asia and
Africa. The European countries he visited are Italy,
France, England, and the Provence. It was on his second
visit to Italy that he died at Rome. He wrote for his living and by way of compensation to his hosts. He was a
philosopher, excellent mathematician, clever poet, and
highly subjective writer. In the domain of philology he
brought to the knowledge of Christian Europe the works
of his great predecessors, and if he was not a very original
grammarian, he was at least a clear-sighted exegete. His
Biblical commentaries are held in high esteem.

Concerning Rashi and Ibn Ezra see also chap. XI, pp.
206-7, and chap. XII, p. 220.

⁹⁴ At this point I think it well to give once for all a summing up of Talmudic literature. The Talmud is the united
mass of the documents and texts of the oral law. It comprises the Mishnah and the Gemara, the latter being called
also Talmud. The Mishnah, a collection in six parts and
forty-nine treatises, is the work of numerous generations
of scholars. Its final redaction (setting aside somewhat
later additions) was made by Judah the Saint, or Rabbi
(about 150-210). The texts not incorporated by Rabbi are

called Baraitas. The Gemara is the commentary and the development of the Mishnah, which it follows step by step, in discussing it and completing its statements. There are two Gemara collections: one elaborated in Palestine under the influence of R. Johanan (199-279) and terminated toward the end of the fourth century, which is called the Palestinian or Jerusalem Talmud; the other drawn up in Babylonia under the influence of Rab and of Samuel (third century), and brought to a conclusion about 500 through the initiative of R. Ashi and his disciples; this is called the Babylonian Talmud. The latter covers the greater part of the Mishnah. It is by far the more important of the two Talmuds from the juridic point of view, and it is the one that has been the chief subject of studies and commentaries. The Talmud comprises two elements: the Halakah, "rule of conduct," legislation, and the Haggadah, "exposition," which embraces non-Halakic exegesis, history, legend, profane learning, etc. The scholars whose discussions are given in the Mishnah are called Tannaim, and those who figure only in the Gemara, Amoraim.

[95] See Appendix II, pp. 232-4.

[96] See p. 91.

[97] Hananel ben Hushiel, of Kairuan, first half of the eleventh century, commented upon the Talmud and the Pentateuch.

[98] This false notion gained currency through the existence of Responsa addressed by Nathan to a certain Solomon ben Isaac: but this Solomon is an Italian. See Vogelstein and Rieger, *Geschichte der Juden in Rom*, I, pp. 366 *et seq*. For further information concerning Nathan ben Jehiel, see Note 121. With regard to recurring names for different individuals—the plague of Jewish literature—it should be said that a French rabbi named Solomon ben Isaac lived about a century after Rashi, who corresponded with R. Tam. He has been confounded with his illustrious predecessor of the same name. See Gross, *Gallia judaica*, p. 34. Buber, Introduction to the *Sefer ha-Orah*, p. 13.

[99] See Notes 37 and 38.

[100] Another name for the Sadduceans, from their chief Boëthus (first century of the Common Era).

[101] Psalm lxxxi. 5, which refers to the new moon. Now, in every case at least two witnesses are necessary.

[102] Lev. xxiii. 40.

[103] Ex. xv. 2.

[104] " And shalt burn with fire the city " (Deut. xiii. 17).

[105] Sukkah 32b. These references placed in parentheses in Rashi's commentary are the work of the printers, who adopted the conventional division into folios. Rashi refers only to the treatise or chapter, at most simply saying " above," or " below."

[106] It is the Latin " scopae."

[107] Mal. i. 13.

[108] Lev. i. 2.

[109] Is. lxi. 8.

[110] A city of Judea, called also Tower of Simon.

[111] Fifth chapter of Hullin, 79a.

[112] The French toile, curtain.

[113] Concerning Hananel, see Note 97. R. Isaac b. Jacob al-Fasi (the initials form Rif) was born in 1013 near Fez, whence his name. In 1088 he went to Spain, where he directed the important school of Lucena. He died in 1103, lamented by all his fellow-citizens. Besides Responsa, he left the " Halakot," or " Little Talmud," which is a pruning down of the entire Talmud, so as to present only what is useful for establishing the norm, deduced by Alfasi himself. It is an important work, which still enjoys great authority. I have already remarked (Note 53) that the Rashi commentary was abridged to make it fit the text of Rif.

[114] In these words Rashi displaces another reading.

[115] Parasang is a Persian measure equivalent to 5250 metres, a fact of which Rashi seems to have been ignorant.

[116] According to Hagigah 13a.

[117] In the first case it refers to Ahriman, the spirit of evil, in the second, to Ormuzd, the spirit of good among the Persians. Lillit in Oriental mythology is a female demon, who wanders at night and attacks chiefly children.

[118] Isaac ben Judah, his master *par excellence*. Concerning Rashi's teachers see chap. I, p. 29; chap. II, pp. 49 *et seq.*; chap. III, p. 58, etc.

[119] Dan. iii. 1.

[120] David Ibn Abi Zimra (Radbaz), rabbi of Cairo, who died, it is said, at Safed in 1589 at the age of 110 years. He left an important collection of Responsa.

[121] Nathan ben Jehiel, of Rome, born about 1035, died in the first years of the twelfth century, author of the Aruk, a highly valued Talmudic dictionary, in which he explains the words of Talmudic and Midrashic literature, as well as the Halakic and Haggadic passages presenting difficulties. The numerous quotations are no less valuable than the explanations. Concerning Alfasi, see Note 113.

[122] Quoted from Bezalel Ashkenazi, who lived in Egypt (died in 1530). He compiled a Talmudic collection called *Shitta Mekubezet*, in which he gathered together extracts from French, Spanish, and other rabbis. Before him Isaac ben Sheshet (see Note 150) had said: "The greatest light that has come to us from France is Rashi. Without his commentary, the Talmud would be a closed book" (Responsa, No. 394).

[123] Menahem ben Zerah (about 1312-1385), son of a Jew expelled from France, wrote in Spain a Talmudic manual entitled *Zedah la-Derek*.

[124] Concerning Rashi's correspondents see chap. II, pp. 51-2, and chap. III, p. 57.

[125] See chap. I, p. 20, and chap. III, p. 56.

[126] See chap. III, p. 67.

[127] And not, as has been supposed, that of Cavaillon, in the county Venaissin, where, possibly, there were not yet any Jews, and where, at all events, Rashi was not known, as was the case throughout the south of France, until after his death.

[128] An application, according to the Talmud, of Eccl. ii. 14.

[129] This resumé is taken from Epstein on Shemaiah, in

Monatsschrift, XLI, also that of *Sefer ha-Orah*. Concerning the Machirites, see chap. I, p. 29, and chap. II, p. 52; concerning Shemaiah, chap. XI, pp. 186-7. The three communities are sometimes called by the initials of their names, "communities of Shum" (שו״ם)

In connection with the *Sefer ha-Pardes* must be mentioned the work bearing the title of *Likkute ha-Pardes* (Extracts from Paradise), a compilation edited in Italy by the disciples of Isaiah da Trani.

[130] See chap. IV, p. 84.

[131] L. Wogue, *Histoire de la Bible et de l'exégèse biblique*, pp. 254-5.

[132] See chap. IX, pp. 171-2.

[133] See p. 162.

[134] Rameru, or Ramerupt, situated six miles from Troyes on a tributary of the Aube. Of old it formed an entire county, proof of which is furnished by the ditches surrounding it and the ruins of a castellated stronghold. At the present day it is the chief city of the Departement de l'Aube.

[135] The sort of literature designated by this word will be defined later on, pp. 191-2.

[136] Chap. VI, p. 125.

[137] Concerning the Biblical exegesis of Samuel ben Meïr see pp. 196-7.

[138] See Note 91.

[139] It has been said that "Tossafot" signifies "supplements to Rashi;" this is not true, but it is noteworthy that the expression is open to such a misconstruction.

[140] Dampierre on the Aube, at present part of the canton of Rameru, counted, after the twelfth century, among the most important lordships in the region.

[141] The name "Morel," customary among English Jews, corresponds to the Hebrew name "Samuel."

[142] See pp. 202-3.

[143] The numeric value of the letters composing the word *Gan* in Hebrew is 53, the number of Pentateuch lessons in the annual cycle.

[144] See chap. VII, pp. 157-8.

[145] Concerning Rashi and Ibn Ezra, see chap. VI, p. 131.

[146] David Kimhi (1160-1235), of Narbonne, a philosopher, a follower of Maimonides, a grammarian, and an exegete, who popularized the works of the Spaniards by his Biblical commentaries, his grammar, and his dictionary. He enjoyed and still enjoys a deserved reputation for clearness and simplicity.

[147] Moses ben Nahman, also called Bonastruc da Porta, born at Gerona in 1195, was a Talmudist, Kabbalist, philosopher, and physician. In 1263 he carried on a disputation at Barcelona with the apostate Pablo Christiano. On this account he went to live in Palestine, where he died in 1270. His was one of the most original personalities in Spanish Judaism.

[148] Solomon ben Abraham ben Adret (1235-1310), born at Barcelona, rabbi and head of an influential school there. The extent of his knowledge as well as his moderation won for him a wide reputation, proof of which is afforded by his intervention as arbiter in the quarrel between the partisans and the adversaries of Maimonides, and by his numerous Responsa, of which about three thousand have been published. Besides, he wrote Talmudic commentaries and casuistic collections.

[149] Asher ben Jehiel, disciple of Meïr of Rothenburg, born about 1250, died in 1327 at Toledo, where he was rabbi. Besides numerous and important Responsa he wrote Talmudic commentaries and a compendium of the Talmud bearing his name.

[150] His initials read Ribash (1336-1408). He exercised rabbinical functions in several cities of Spain. After the persecutions of 1391, he went to Algiers, where he was appointed rabbi. He was well-informed in philosophy, but he owes his great reputation chiefly to his Talmudic knowledge, as is proved by his numerous Responsa.

[151] Rashbaz, born in 1361 on Majorca, of a family originally from the Provence. At first he practiced medicine, but, reduced to poverty by the persecutions of 1391, he resigned

himself, not without scruples, to accepting the emoluments
of a rabbi. He died in 1444 at Algiers, where he had been
the co-worker, then the successor, of Ribash. He is known
chiefly for his commentaries and his Responsa. The passage
in question is taken from these Responsa, No. 394. See also
Note 122.

[152] See chap. II, p. 31, and chap. IV, p. 80.

[153] See chap. II, pp. 31-2.

[154] The daughter of Solomon Luria married a brother of
the famous Talmudist of Cracow, Moses Isserles (1530-
1572). I will add that the families of Treves, Pollak, Hel-
ler, and Katzenellenbogen also maintain that they are connected with Rashi. On the descendants of Rashi, see Epstein, *Mishpahat Lurie we-Kohen-Zedek*, in *Ha-Goren*, I,
Appendix.

[155] See chap. II, p. 37.

[156] This defective edition was replaced by a good critical
edition by David Rosin (Breslau, 1881).

[157] L. Wogue, *Histoire de la Bible et de l'exégèse biblique*,
p. 319.

[158] Abraham Geiger, born in 1810 at Frankfort, died at
Berlin in 1874, one of the finest Jewish scholars of the nineteenth century. His prolific activity was exerted in all
provinces of Jewish history and literature. Besides works
upon the Talmud, the poets, the philosophers, and the
exegetes of the middle ages, he wrote numerous articles in
two journals, which he successively edited. Theologian
and distinguished preacher, he promoted the reform of the
Jewish cult in Germany.

[159] Wolf Heidenheim (1757-1832), Talmudist, Hebrew
scholar, and editor. He deserves the sobriquet of the Henri
Estienne of Hebrew letters. The commentary in which he
defends Rashi is entitled *Habanat ha-Mikra*. Only the beginning, up to Gen. xliii. 16, has appeared.

[160] Isaac Hirsch Weiss (1815-1905), professor at the Bet
ha-Midrash of Vienna, wrote many studies scattered through
two literary magazines edited by him successively, and also
an important History of Jewish Tradition, in five volumes.

[161] Solomon Judah Rapoport, born in 1790, died rabbi of Prague in 1867. Together with Zunz, he was the founder of modern Jewish science. A distinguished man of letters, he was known above all for his biographies of celebrated rabbis, for historic and archaeologic studies, and for an unfinished encyclopedia.

[162] Zechariah Frankel, born at Prague in 1801, after 1854 director of the Seminary at Breslau, where he died in 1875. He left historic studies on the Mosaic-Talmudic law, introductions to the Septuagint, the Jerusalem Talmud, and the Mishnah, and numerous critical and historical works in the Programs of the Seminary and in the *Monatsschrift*, a magazine edited by him from 1851 on.

INDEX

INDEX

Aaron ben Joseph, Biblical commentary by, 199.

Aaron the Elder, correspondent of Rashi, 57.

Abelard, scholastic, alluded to, 54.

Abodah Zarah, laazim bearing on, 99.

Abrabanel. *See* Isaac Abrabanel.

Abraham ben Garton, printer of Rashi's commentary, 214.

Abraham ben Jehiel, fellow-student of Rashi, 52.

Abraham ben Meïr, fellow-student of Rashi, 52

Abraham ben Nathan, Tossafist, 194.

Abraham Ibn Ezra, contrasted with Rashi, 76, 79, 131-2; alluded to, 91; obscurity of, 95; correspondent of Jacob Tam, 190; combats Rashi, 206-7; poem by, on Rashi, 206-7; Luzzatto on, 220; data about, 252, n. 93.

Abraham the Just, Rashi's companion in Paradise, 71.

Absalom, subject of Psalm IX, 96.

Africa, Northern, the scholars of, make use of Responsa, 160.

Agriculture, pursued by Jews, 20.

Aḥa, Gaon, cited by Rashi, 83, 248, n. 46.

Akdamot Millin, poem, author of, 244, n. 19.

Alexius, Saint, life of, alluded to, 102.

Alfasi. *See* Isaac Alfasi.

Amalek, subject of Psalm IX, 96.

Amoraim the, the generations of, distinguished by Rashi, 150; term explained, 253, n. 94.

" Amphitryon, The." *See Ha-Parnas.*

Apocrypha, the, not known to Rashi, 83.

Arabic, Rashi supposed to have known, 80, 82.

Arabs, the, and the sciences, 81-2; stimulate grammatical studies, 127.

Aramaic, handled easily by Rashi, 97; used by Rashi, 129.

Aristotle, alluded to, 76, 93.

Arles, alluded to, 243, n. 2.

Ashi, redactor of the Talmud, 253, n. 94.

Asher ben Jehiel (Asheri, Rosh), on Samson of Sens, 193; influenced by Rashi, 209; data about, 257, n. 149.

Asher ha-Levi, martyr, 66.

Asheri. *See* Asher ben Jehiel.

Asia, the Jews of, influenced by the Babylonian Exile, 108.

Astronomy, supposed to be known by Rashi, 80, 82.

Atonement, eve of the Day of, poem for, 176-8.

Austrasia, early settlement of Jews in, 18.

Autobiographies, Jewish, paucity of, 31.

Auto-da-fé, at Blois, 189; under St. Louis, 217.

Auxerre, the " wise men " of, correspondents of Rashi, 57, 128.

Azriel ben Nathan, fellow-student of Rashi, 52.

Azulaï, bibliographer, on Rashi, 95.

Baba Batra, Talmudical treatise, commentary on, 97.

Baba Batra 73a, as interpreted by Rashi, 153-5.

Babylon, the scholars of, make use of Responsa, 160.

Babylonian academies, the, the decline of, 28.

Babylonian Exile, the, the influence of, 108.

Babylonian influences in the West, 27.

Bacon, Roger, alluded to, 201.

Bacher, W., on Rashi, 221.

Bahya. See Beḥaia ben Asher.

Baptism. *See* Conversions; Converts.

Bar-sur-Aube, fairs held at, 35.

Baraitas, the, Rashi on, 150; term explained, 253, n. 94.

Barcelona, alluded to, 71, 81.

Bartolocci, bibliographer, on the name of Rashi, 33.

Baruch ben Isaac, casuist, 193.

Basnage, historian, on the name of Rashi, 34; quoted, 57.

Beḥaia ben Asher, uses Rashi's Bible commentary, 208.

Bellassez, daughter of Rashi, 62, 245, n. 24.

Bellette, renders ritual decisions, 62.

Ben Sira, the wisdom of, how known to Rashi, 83.

Benjamin ben Abraham Anaw, uses Rashi's commentary, 206.

Benjamin of Tudela, traveller, alluded to, 34.